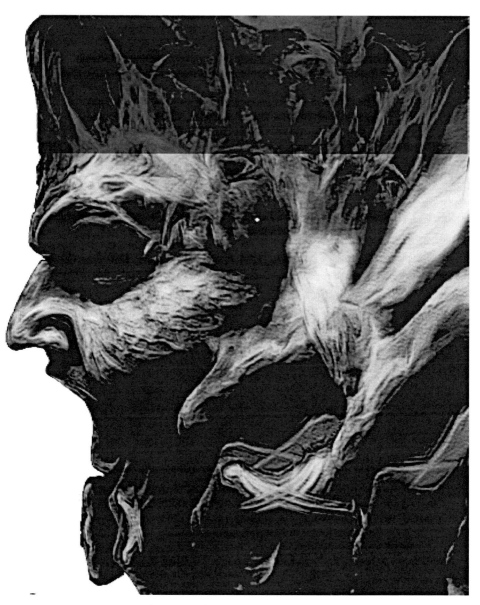

BEN REDMOND

Visit Ben Redmond's website at www.variousparables.com
Visit Samizdat Creative's website at www.samizdatcreative.com

ISBN-10 0982612451
ISBN-13 9780982612453

Published in association with Westwinds Community Church, 1000 Robinson Road, Jackson, MI 49203

Published by Samizdat Creative, 5441 South Knox Court, Littleton, CO 80123.
All scriptures used in this Atlas are taken from the NIV translation unless otherwise indicated.

This book was written primarily for the people of Westwinds Community Church in Jackson, Michigan. It is part of a series of similar books called "Teaching Atlases," which supplement the sermons during the weekend worship services. They are part study-guide, part reminder, part artifact.

Additional Atlases can be obtained through the office of Westwinds Community Church on a host of other topics.

Ben is also available for guest teaching, speaking, or youth ministry consulting. You can reach him at ben.redmond@westwinds.org.

The set-up costs of each Atlas are privately donated by a Westwinds' parishioner, thus enabling extensive self-publishing at a reasonable cost. The proceeds from each Atlas are designated by the donor for a specific project—such as installing wells in developing countries, providing artistic and educational scholarships for children, or financially supporting pastors and missionaries around the world.

If you would like to donate to the Atlas project, please contact info@westwinds.org

ACKNOWLEDGMENTS

Special thanks to:

My Dad, Mark Redmond, for his grammatical editing. He is the true writer in the family, and his feedback made this book better.

Corey Grazul for his feedback and his work on the discussion questions that appear at the end of each section.

Caleb Seeling, Julie Little, and the team at Samizdat Creative for their work as the primary editors of this book.

Mel Evans for her work on the cover design and book layout.

Becky Veydt for her work on the elements of spiritual formation that appear at the end of each section.

DEDICATIONS

This atlas is dedicated to Susie Redmond for her deep faith and hope in the true God of the world. Her understanding of God allowed her to live a remarkable life during her time on earth. Through pain, exile, and eventually death, she remained completely convinced of God's great love and mercy.

This atlas is also dedicated to the leadership team at Student Journey. I am lucky to be surrounded by such Godly, passionate, and talented people. Thank you for loving God, loving each other, and loving our students.

TABLE OF CONTENTS

Nahum:
The Cobblestone Translation

Chapter One

This message concerning Nineveh came as a vision to Nahum,
Who lived in Elkosh.
It's a poem to the divine warrior.

The Lord is a jealous God who punishes;
The Lord avenges and is furious.
He takes revenge on all who oppose him,
And He stays angry with His enemies.

The Lord is slow to anger and great in power.
He's powerful, but it's a patient power.
Still, no one gets by with anything.

The Lord has His way in the whirlwind and in the storm,
And the clouds are the dust of His feet.
At His command the oceans dry up,
And the rivers disappear.
The Bashan and Carmel mountains shrivel,
The Lebanon orchards shrivel.

The mountains shake in front of Him,
And the hills melt.
The earth heaves before Him.
The world and all who live in it shake with fear.

Who can face such towering anger?
        Who can stand up to this fierce rage?
His fury is poured out like fire,
        And his fury shatters boulders.

The Lord is good, giving protection in times of trouble.
        He protects those who take refuge in Him.

But with an overwhelming flood
        He will completely destroy Nineveh;
He will pursue His enemies into darkness.

The Lord will completely destroy anyone making plans against him.
        He will destroy you with one blow; He won't need to strike twice!

Like thorns they are entangled,
        Like drunkards they are drunk;
They will be burned up quickly like dry weeds.

Someone has come from Nineveh who plots evil against the Lord,
        And gives wicked advice.

This is what the Lord says: "Even though you're on top of the world,
        You will be destroyed and disappear.
O my people, I have punished you before,
        But I will not punish you again with Assyrian oppression.
"Now I will free you from their control and tear away your chains."

And this is what the Lord says concerning the Assyrians in Nineveh:
> "You're the end of the line.
I will destroy your idols and metal images that are in the temple of our gods.
> I will make your grave, for you are worthless."

Look, there on the mountains, the feet of one who brings good news,
> Who proclaims peace!
Celebrate your festivals, O people of Judah. Worship and recommit to God,
> For your wicked enemies will never invade your land again.
They have been completely destroyed!

CHAPTER TWO

Your enemy is coming to crush you, Nineveh.
> Man the fort!
>> Watch the road!
>>> Dress for battle!
>>>> Call out your forces!

Destroyers have destroyed God's people and ruined their vines,
> But the Lord will restore the honor of Jacob.

Shields flash red in the sunlight;
> The warriors are clad in scarlet.
Watch as their glittering chariots move into position;
> A spiked forest of brandished spears.

The chariots race madly through the streets,
> And rush wildly through the squares.
They look like torches; they run like lightning.

The Assyrian king rallies his men,
       But they stumble on the way.
They dash to the city wall,
       And the defense is prepared.
The river gates are thrown open,
       And the palace is destroyed.

Nineveh's exile has been decreed.
       The slave girls moan like doves and beat their breasts,
           Because they are sad.

Nineveh is like a pool, and its water is draining away.
       "Stop! Stop!" they cry, but no one turns back.

Take the silver! Take the gold!
       There's no end to Nineveh's treasures.

Nineveh is robbed, ruined, and destroyed.
       Hearts sink,
           Knees fold,
                 Stomachs retch,
                      And every face grows pale.

Where is the famous and fierce Assyrian lion,
       And the place where they feed their young?
It was a place where people _ like lions and their cubs _
       Walked freely and without fear.

The lion tore in pieces enough for his cubs,
  Killed for his lionesses, filling his lairs with the kill
And his dens with the prey.

"See, I am your enemy," says the Lord of Heaven's armies.
  "I will burn up your chariots in smoke,
And the sword will kill your young lions.
  Never again will you plunder conquered nations,
And the voice of your messengers shall be heard no more."

CHAPTER THREE

Woe to the city of blood –
  Full of lies,
    Crammed with wealth,
      Addicted to violence!

Hear the sound of whips and the noise of the wheels.
  Hear horses galloping and chariots clattering wildly.

Horsemen charge with bright sword and glittering spear.
  Piles of dead, heaps of corpses,
So many bodies that people stumble over them.

All because of the endless lust of the prostitute, the mistress of sorceries.
  She was charming and a lover of magic.
She hade nations slaves with her prostitution and her witchcraft.

"I am your enemy, whore Nineveh",
        Says the Lord of Heaven's armies.
"I will pull your dress up over your face
        And show all the earth your nakedness and shame."

I will pelt you with dung and make a fool of you.
        I will make people stare at you: "Slut on exhibit!"

All who see you will shrink back and say,
        "Nineveh is wasted. Where are the mourners?
Does anyone regret your destruction?"

Are you any better than the city of Thebes,
        Proudly invincible on the Nile River?
The river was her defense; the waters were like a wall around her.
        Cush and Egypt gave her endless strength; Put and Libya supported her.

But Thebes was captured and went into captivity.
        Her babies smashed to death in public view on the streets,
Her prize leaders auctioned off, and all of her leaders put in chains.

Expect the same treatment, Nineveh.
        You will also be drunk; you will be hidden;
You will look for a place safe from the enemy.
        All your defenses are like fig trees with ripe fruit.
If they are shaken, they fall into the mouth of the eater.

Look at your troops _ they are women!
  The gates of your land are wide open to your enemies;
Enemy fire will burn you up.

Get enough water before the long war begins.
  Make your defenses strong!
Go into the pits to trample clay, and pack it into molds,
  Making bricks to repair the walls.

But the fire will devour you; the sword will kill you.
  The enemy will consume you like locusts, devouring everything they see.
There will be no escape, even if you multiply like swarming locusts.

Your traders are more than the stars in the sky.
  But like a swarm of locusts,
They strip the land and then fly away.
  Your commanders are like swarming locusts,
And your generals like great grasshoppers
  Settling on the fences on a cold day.
When the sun comes up, they fly away,
  And no one knows where they have gone.

Your shepherds are asleep, O Assyrian king;
  Your princes lie dead in the dust.
Your people are scatter and lost,
  And there is no one to bring them back.
There is no healing for your wound; your injury is fatal.
  Everyone who hears about you will applaud.
Where can anyone be found who has not suffered from your endless cruelty?

INTRODUCTION

Confession: I don't understand God sometimes.

Ok, it's been about two minutes since I wrote those words. I am still alive, and I don't have leprosy.

Don't get me wrong: I believe in God, I just don't understand Him.

That's why I normally stick to the Jesus version. Most of what I know about Jesus comes from the Second Testament. I love reading about Jesus as he does wonderful things like heal people, show compassion, perform miracles, and talk about love.

I understand Jesus. Jesus makes sense to me. I understand why he came, how he lived, and what he wants me to do. Following Jesus means loving people, turning the other cheek, and obeying the teachings in the Bible. The Jesus way isn't always easy to do but it is easy to understand. He became human, giving us an example of how to be human ourselves.

God the Father is completely different. Most of what I know about God comes from the First Testament. He often seems to act in anger, judging His enemies, judging His people, and threatening people with punishment.

God doesn't make sense to me. I am not sure I know what He wants or can live the way He requires. I am terrified that I might make Him angry. The God way is impossible to understand and even harder to follow. Doesn't the Bible even say that "His ways are not our ways"? There is a big difference between God in the First Testament and Jesus in the Second Testament.

Enter Nahum. Nahum shares a vision from God about how God is going to wipe out another nation. God's words through Nahum are mean, aggressive, and sometimes just horrible. If Nahum were a movie, it would definitely be rated "R."

The good news is that nobody reads Nahum. Scholars agree that Nahum is the least read, quoted, or studied book of the Bible. Nahum presents us with versions of God that seem to be conflicting. In Nahum, God is a patient warrior and a jealous lover. He is an angry judge, and a comforting avenger. Like God, Nahum is just too hard to understand.

This is precisely why we are discussing Nahum at the Winds.

> Have you ever felt uncomfortable with the conflicting versions of God?

> Have you ever struggled with God's anger and violence?

> Have you ever wondered what God wants from you?

If you have wrestled with any of these ideas of God, then this book is for you. Understanding God the Father is important. In fact, you cannot appreciate Jesus fully without knowing something about the nature of his Father. Nahum will require you to wade deep into some very tough issues, but it will give you the opportunity to explore who God is and what really matters to Him.

God is not who you have imagined Him to be.

He is more…much more.

This book is made up of several components:

1. **A Cobblestone Translation**

    The Cobblestone Bible is a translation project wherein the most accurate and informative renderings of phrases and word choices have been selected from several versions of Scripture and pieced together to form a user-specific and user-friendly rendition. This Cobblestone is taken from the following versions:

    New Living Translation
    The Message
    English Standard Version
    New Revised Standard Version
    American Standard Version
    New King James Version
    New International Version
    The New Century Version

    We recommend reading the Cobblestone Translation in conjunction with the Bible you normally study.

2. **Articles and Sermons on Nahum**

    These are the individual chapters that help make sense of the big issues and themes presented in Nahum. While these chapters deal primarily with who God is and how we respond, they also touch on a wide range of other issues. These chapters are important to help us apply the themes of Nahum to our everyday lives.

3. **Discussion Questions**

    At the end of each section are several questions for discussion. These questions are designed for you and your friends to discuss in a satellite or over coffee. We encourage you to use them as conversation starters, allowing the Spirit to take you deeper.

4. **Elements of Spiritual Formation**

    We no longer want to think that Christian spirituality is only about learning. Until we apply what we know, we don't really know it…we've only heard it. To that end, we have included spiritual disciplines (habits and practices) to help you apply what you learn in each section.

With these tools, my great hope is that you will courageously explore the complex nature of our great God in a way that changes you.

Together,

Ben

SECTION ONE:
Nahum 1:1-14

Nahum Chapter One:
The Cobblestone Translation

This message concerning Nineveh came as a vision to Nahum,
       Who lived in Elkosh.
It's a poem to the divine warrior.

The Lord is a jealous God who punishes;
       The Lord avenges and is furious.
He takes revenge on all who oppose him,
       And He stays angry with His enemies.

The Lord is slow to anger and great in power.
       He's powerful, but it's a patient power.
Still, no one gets by with anything.

The Lord has His way in the whirlwind and in the storm,
       And the clouds are the dust of His feet.
At His command the oceans dry up,
       And the rivers disappear.
The Bashan and Carmel mountains shrivel,
       The Lebanon orchards shrivel.

The mountains shake in front of Him,
         And the hills melt.
The earth heaves before Him.
         The world and all who live in it shake with fear.

Who can face such towering anger?
         Who can stand up to this fierce rage?
His fury is poured out like fire,
         And his fury shatters boulders.

The Lord is good, giving protection in times of trouble.
         He protects those who take refuge in Him.

But with an overwhelming flood
         He will completely destroy Nineveh;
He will pursue His enemies into darkness.

The Lord will completely destroy anyone making plans against him.
         He will destroy you with one blow; He won't need to strike twice!

Like thorns they are entangled,
         Like drunkards they are drunk;
they will be burned up quickly like dry weeds.

Someone has come from Nineveh who plots evil against the Lord,
         And gives wicked advice.

This is what the Lord says: "Even though you're on top of the world,
      You will be destroyed and disappear.
O my people, I have punished you before,
      But I will not punish you again with Assyrian oppression.
"Now I will free you from their control and tear away your chains."

And this is what the Lord says concerning the Assyrians in Nineveh:
      "You're the end of the line.
I will destroy your idols and metal images that are in the temple of our gods.
      I will make your grave, for you are worthless."

Look, there on the mountains, the feet of one who brings good news,
      Who proclaims peace!
Celebrate your festivals, O people of Judah. Worship and recommit to God,
      For your wicked enemies will never invade your land again.
They have been completely destroyed!

ben redmond

CHAPTER ONE:
Flabby Habby

When I was in fourth grade, I was a wimpy kid with a big mouth. This combination never served me well.

The resident school bully during my elementary years was Jeff Habbijanic, labeled "Flabby Habby" by those he tormented. He was one grade and one hundred pounds ahead of me.

As the biggest mouth in our small band of weaklings, I took it upon myself to speak against Flabby Habby's ways of oppression. I would secretly mock him. I would write anonymous notes. I would dream with my friends of a day when his bullying would end. My words eventually earned me a punishment with a catchy name: "purple nurple." If you have never had a purple nurple, please know that the name is certainly more festive than the experience.

I often warned Flabby Habby that if the bullying didn't stop, I would tell my dad. No self-respecting fourth grade boy wants to tell his dad about purple nurples, but that action was my only hope.

My dad was as big as he was scary. His pectoral muscles could move independently like Arnold Schwarzenegger's in *Conan the Barbarian*. My dad was also loving and protective. His presence always made me feel secure.

One day, my dad stopped the bullying for good.

School had just ended for the day, and The other weaklings and I were hiding from Flabby Habby on the playground. From our hiding spot, I saw him tormenting some other fourth graders, and I decided to act.

Picking up a rock, I threw it at his head.

I mentioned that I was a skinny weakling. I should also mention that I was a very slow runner. As it turns out, though, I had a really great arm!

Flabby Habby turned around like a giant troll and with a grunt of rage, began to run toward me. I decided that right then was a good time to head for home.

Sprinting the few blocks from the school to my house, I could feel Flabby Habby's breath on my neck. As I grabbed the door handle, his massive troll hands closed around my scrawny neck.

What a way to go.

As I braced myself for the inevitable beating, the back door of my house flew open.

It was my dad.

From that point, everything seemed to happen in slow motion, and I swear I heard the theme from the *Rocky* movies. My dad angrily explained to Flabby Habby what would happen if he put his hands on me again. I will never forget the feeling of standing with my dad as our conquered enemy faded into the distance.

Dealing with a bully is a lot easier when Dad is on your side.

Nahum lived in similar, yet far more serious, circumstances. During the seventh century B.C., the ancient Near East was completely dominated by the sadistic and brutal nation of Assyria.

We don't know much about Nahum. We do know that he was originally from the northern part of Israel, but the Assyrians had destroyed his hometown. When he wrote this prophecy, he was living in the southern part of Israel. He had witnessed the Assyrian cruelty first hand.

He felt the oppression.

His people suffered.

His hometown was gone.

It was time to respond.

Nahum certainly responded, but not with force or power. He stood up to the bully with words. The fresh and descriptive quality of his writing indicates that Nahum was a poet. In fact, many scholars refer to Nahum as the "poet laureate" of the prophetic writers. But the origin of the words, not the quality, makes them remarkable.

Nahum's response wasn't really *his* response. The words come in the form of a vision from God. Specifically, this vision was a war oracle, a dream from God about the destruction of a bully.

God gave Nahum a vision of the complete destruction of the Assyrian Empire. And this dream wasn't to be kept close to the vest. Nahum was told to publicly share what he had seen.

God gave many prophets in Scripture a variation of this message:

"God is angry and about to destroy you. Turn back now and you will be spared."

Nahum's message was a bit different:

"God is angry and about to destroy you. The end."

The message of Nahum does not carry a single note of hope for the Assyrians: no mention of repentance or offer of forgiveness, only the guarantee of judgment and destruction.

As with any evil regime, the Assyrians didn't tolerate comments from the cheap seats. Nahum's prophecy was so graphic and violent that some scholars believe he used a pseudonym to protect himself from retaliation. Like me, Nahum might have been the biggest mouth in a small band of weaklings.

Regardless of whether Nahum was his historical name, its meaning still has significance. Depending upon the context, Nahum can mean either *comforte*r or *avenger*.

Nahum delivers the message of God, who, like my dad, stands simultaneously in protection and opposition. As "Comforting Avenger," God brings hope to the oppressed and fear to the oppressor.

Because of Nahum's aggressive style, we could easily think of him as an optimistic patriot who wrote anonymous threats to the Assyrians. This mental picture does not work for one reason:

These words were not Nahum's words.

Nahum didn't express his individual plan of attack. He relayed a vision *from God* that was based completely on what Nahum believed *about God*.

God was present with His people; in the end, the bully didn't stand a chance.

CHAPTER 2:
Monsters

Every kid believes in monsters at some point.

Both of my kids went through their "monster" phase. These monsters lived in Kayla's closet and in Ethan's dreams. I repeatedly tried to reassure them that the monsters were not real, but I never really convinced them.

Then one day the monsters disappeared.

With no fanfare, my kids quietly outgrew the monster phase. I even tried hiding in their rooms and making monster noises (one of the Biblical responsibilities given to fathers), but nothing worked. Kayla and Ethan just weren't afraid anymore.

Recently I had a conversation with my ten-year-old daughter Kayla. Kayla is a redhead.

Smart + Social + Stubborn = Redhead.

Kayla doesn't just ask questions; she demands answers. With my son Ethan, I can change subjects and let his ADD do the rest. Not so with Kayla. She stays on course until she gets an answer that makes sense to her.

On this particular day, we were discussing slavery. The conversation went something like this:

"Dad, what is slavery?"

"Slavery is people owning people."

"We learned about it in school today. People owning people is wrong."

"You're right honey – it is a horrible thing."

"Well, I'm really glad it's over now."

"What?"

"Slavery. I'm glad slavery is over. It is over, right?"

"Kind of."

"Kind of? How do you 'kind of' own people? Is it over or not?"

For the next thirty minutes I explained modern-day slavery to my daughter. I told her about the over twenty-seven million people still in slavery today. We talked about people like Zach Hunter, a teenage abolitionist, who are trying to stop it. We even prayed, asking God to free the slaves. Watching Kayla head upstairs with tears in her eyes, I thought about the other conversations that are coming:

Hitler and the Holocaust,

Stalin and the Soviet Union,

the Rwandan genocide,

Saddam Hussein's mass graves,

sex trafficking.

I realized that each conversation would open my daughter's eyes to new fears. Each new reality of human suffering and injustice would add weight to her little heart. She couldn't possibly be the same after hearing these stories.

The monsters had returned.

We have a few years at best of monster-free living. Once we are old enough to understand either history or current events, a new kind of monster emerges. These new monsters don't live under beds, but we all wish that they did.

In the seventh century B.C., the Assyrians were the new monsters. Kings like Sennacherib and Assurbanipal led Assyria to unrivaled world domination. Assyrian technology, architecture, and military strategy were unmatched.

Assyrian affluence led Nahum to refer to their wealth as "endless." Gods and goddesses such as Assur and Marduk required other people's stuff as their primary offering. The Assyrian army systematically "borrowed" everything from everyone until the government was forced to build additional temples just to hold the leftovers.

What truly set the Assyrians apart was their sadistic brutality. Assyrian kings went out of their way to make sure their cruelty was recorded through written and pictorial descriptions. Here are just a few of the things we know about Assyrian brutality:

> They used "scorched earth" warfare, completely destroying the environment of any city they conquered.

> They took hundreds of thousands of slaves. The youngest and most attractive women were given to successful soldiers as "sex toys."

They would require a mother to hold her young son while they cut out his eyes and tongue. They would also cut off a child's hands, feet, and testicles while he was in his mother's arms. They would place the head of the child on a pole, which the mother would carry until it rotted away.

> I flayed the skin from as many nobles as had rebelled against me and draped their skins over the pile of corpses…I cut off the heads of their fighters and built with them a tower before my city. I burnt their children…I cut off their arms and legs. I made one pile of the living and one of the dead. I hung their heads on trees outside my palace. **King Assurbanipal**

Understanding the depth of Assyrian brutality helps us understand the depth of God's anger. The Assyrians were not simply found guilty of jaywalking. They had tortured and brutalized all of God's creation for two hundred and fifty years!

God was angry with these Assyrian monsters for their deep cruelty and injustice toward His entire creation, but He had another motivation.

You see, God had been angry at the Assyrian monsters once before.

One hundred and fifty years before our story, God had asked the prophet Jonah to communicate His anger with the Assyrians. You might know Jonah best for a small encounter he had with a fish, but that was only part of the story. Weary of the Assyrian monsters, God asked Jonah to go to the capital city of Nineveh and tell them to "turn or burn." Nahum had to write down a vision, but Jonah had to take a field trip right down Main Street.

In fear, Jonah ran from God. He also ran because he didn't want to see the monsters rescued.

Eventually Jonah gave the Assyrians God's message of repentance. Remarkably, they actually repented! The Assyrian king at the time called for an end to all violence and false-god worship.

Scripture tells us that this act of repentance brought compassion from God. He gave the Assyrians another chance.

Eventually, however, their desire for conquest outweighed their fear of God. The Assyrians returned to their ways of sadistic brutality, ignoring the warning of Jonah, and again worshipping their false gods.

Assyria revoked its repentance, and the monsters became monsters once again. This is why Nahum's message to Assyria contains no hope for them. By revoking their repentance they made a big mistake:

They took God lightly.

When we revoke our repentance, we take God lightly. We claim to have some better way forward than the one He offers. Sometimes we revoke our repentance intentionally. You might think of this as rebellion. Other times we revoke our repentance accidentally. You might think of this as apathy. In either case we forget that, in a world of monsters, none has more power than the One True God. He will use that power to protect the innocent, but the monsters won't be so lucky.

> "The Lord is slow to anger and great in power; He will not leave the guilty unpunished." **Nahum 1:3**

CHAPTER 3:
This God is Hard to Like

Sometimes our view of God keeps us from understanding important things about Him. For instance, some of us carry the "Art Whitaker" version of God.

When I was a kid, Art Whitaker was an elderly man who attended our church. He was the stereotypical old man, complete with the walker and a top speed of five miles-per-decade. Every Sunday he stood by the front door to hand out candy to the kids as they came to church.

This kind gesture aside, Art was a pretty crabby old man with strict rules for candy recipients. If you ran up the sidewalk toward the building, he became like the "Soup Nazi" from *Seinfeld*: no candy for you.

One Sunday I came bolting up the sidewalk to grab my candy. As I reached for the open hand, Art yanked it back and snarled,

"If you run, you don't get candy."

I wanted candy, and when Art opened his hand for the next kid I grabbed a piece and tried to escape. Art grabbed me by the hair in an attempt to bring me to justice, but I kicked him in the leg and made my escape.

Art Whitaker had rules, and he was one tough Son of a Baptist, but he wasn't very powerful.

Some of us think God is like Art Whitaker. He has rules that He will enforce, but He has to catch us first. Because this God is limited, we make light of Him.

Nahum tells us that this Comforting Avenger is serious business. Listen to Nahum's words about God:

"The LORD is a jealous and
    Avenging God;
The LORD takes vengeance
    And is filled with wrath.
The LORD takes vengeance on his foes
    And maintains his wrath against His enemies." **Nahum 1:2**

These verses need some explanation so that we can view God correctly. Remember, the sin of the Assyrians involved taking God lightly.

Nahum first tells us that this God is jealous. The idea of a jealous God can be hard to understand, because we normally see jealousy in a negative light. Human jealousy can be very petty at times.

> There is the husband who will not trust his wife, though she has been completely faithful to him.

> There is the friend who cannot celebrate your success.

> There is the family member who always celebrates your failures.

However, we would all agree that sometimes jealousy is the appropriate response.

> Imagine catching your teenage daughter at a coffee shop with a middle-aged man. The man explains that he has been talking to your fourteen-year-old in a chat room, and they are now madly in love. He and your daughter have agreed to elope to a country that allows girls her age to marry without parental consent . Also, he has a very suspicious mustache.

Let's assume that you did not beat this man all the way back to his creepy van with the tinted windows. If you stopped to assess your feelings, you would find that you were jealous for your daughter. You would be jealous for the affections that are rightfully yours. You would act swiftly, attempting to remove the pervert and reprogram your daughter's sense of affection.

This is the jealousy of God, which we can trace back directly to His deep love for His created children.

God is jealous for the affection of His created people because it rightly belongs to Him alone. He is also jealous for the well being of His people because He knows they will suffer through disobedience.

The second thing Nahum tells us is that God is an avenger. Three times in this verse Nahum uses the word *avenger* or *vengeance*. As with jealousy, vengeance is difficult to connect with God. Films like *Taken, Law Abiding Citizen,* and *The Edge of Darkness* (not to mention every single Steven Segal movie) give us a picture of the person who has been provoked and is forced to take justice into his own hands. So how are we to understand God as the avenger?

It helps to think of God's vengeance as a response rather than a natural attribute. In other words, God avenges because of His jealousy, not because of His nature. While this distinction might seem like hair splitting, it makes all the difference in the world. God's vengeance and human vengeance always carry different motives. In fact, human vengeance is not capable of pure motive. The avenger is always implicated.

On the television show *24*, Jack Bauer continually finds himself in situations where he must carry out evil in order to sustain the greater good. A recurring theme of the show is his unresolved guilt over his actions.

The human avenger's hands are never clean.

This reality makes the following verse of Scripture incredibly important:

"It is mine to avenge, I will repay." **Deuteronomy 32:35**

The Bible states that vengeance belongs only to God, because only He can avenge with the pure motive of His jealousy. Two phrases in verse two further explain this idea.

Nahum says that God is "filled with wrath." This phrase is best translated, "a master of anger." God is not possessed with rage or controlled by a need for vengeance. He has mastered vengeance and can carry it out in complete purity.

Nahum also says that God "maintains His wrath against His enemies." The word maintain comes from a word used in gardening. "To maintain wrath" means to fight against weeds that kill plants or against foxes that steal grapes. When God says that He maintains His wrath, He gives hope to those facing oppression. Only the Comforting Avenger can handle the responsibility of protecting the innocent and judging the guilty.

This has a very practical application for us today. You cannot play the role of avenger. You might be a victim who has suffered greatly at the hands of another person, but vengeance does not belong to you. In Romans, Paul gives us another way to respond when vengeance seems like the only answer:

"Do not repay anyone evil for evil. Be careful to do what is right in the eyes of everybody. If it is possible, as far as it depends on you, live at peace with everyone. Do not take revenge, my friends, but leave room for God's wrath, for it is written: 'It is mine to avenge; I will repay,' says the Lord. On the contrary: If your enemy is hungry, feed him; if he is thirsty, give him something to drink. In doing this, you will heap burning coals on his head. Do not be overcome with evil, but overcome evil with good." **Romans 12:17-21**

As followers of Jesus, we must let God avenge. Furthermore, we must head in the opposite direction. We have to love and forgive. Interestingly, Paul doesn't say that our forgiveness will make the other person feel great. In fact, he says that act of forgiveness will cause far more pain than any amount of vengeance we could dish out.

Forgiveness is our revenge.

Two of my former students have been best friends since grade school. I'll call them Sally and Cindy. Both Sally and Cindy were raped. A family member raped Sally, and a friend raped Cindy. I've watched them struggle to give up their right for vengeance. A year after her rape, Sally told me,

> "I saw him the other day. For the first time in a year, I didn't wish he were dead."

Forgiveness for Sally doesn't mean that she will ever trust her abuser again, it means that she refuses to take hold of any form of vengeance.

Sally and Cindy are teaching me this truth: revenge is God's, but forgiveness is mine through Jesus.

CHAPTER 4:
Anger Management

As a kid I loved the Incredible Hulk. I watched all the cartoons, read all the comics, and collected all the action figures. My dad and I probably logged one thousand hours playing a game we called "Hulk." Here is how to play "Hulk" with your kids:

1. Let them punch you.
2. Warn them by saying, "Please don't make me angry."
3. When they punch you again, fall down and begin to transform.
4. Chase them around the house.

I will never forget the day my dad allowed me to move up to the real thing.

The Incredible Hulk on TV, starring Bill Bixby and Lou Ferrigno.

If you've only seen the two newer movies, you have not had the full "Hulk experience." Every episode of *The Incredible Hulk* is exactly the same:

David (Bruce) Banner, played by Bill Bixby, wanders into a town. He always wanders because of his horrible secret. His horrible secret also keeps him from having the same girlfriend for consecutive episodes.

Banner gets a job as a clerk in a country store or as a janitor at a factory in this new town. He makes some friends and, to the untrained eye, is settling in quite nicely. Then the trouble comes. Some bad guys harass some innocent people, and Banner tries to intervene. The bad guys jump him and prepare to give him a beating.

At this point Banner looks at the bad guys and says, "Please don't make me angry. You wouldn't like me when I'm angry." The bad guys punch him in the stomach; Banner falls down behind a trash can, and out comes the Incredible Hulk (played by Ferrigno). He smashes the bad guys and destroys a barn or factory in the process. As the action dies down, he turns back to normal and heads for the next town.

What made the Incredible Hulk interesting was that he never went looking for a fight. He would plead with the bad guys, "Please don't make me angry."

> "The LORD is slow to anger
>> And great in power;
> The LORD will not leave
>> The guilty unpunished." **Nahum 1:3**

Nahum says God is slow to anger. This might be the most confusing statement Nahum makes. How is God jealous, vengeful, and slow to anger?

Spoiler alert: Nahum's guarantee of Assyrian destruction does come true. In 612 B.C., the Medes joined forces with the Babylonians to storm the city of Nineveh and end Assyrian dominance.

Not only did it happen; it happened just as Nahum said it would.

Nahum's description of God as slow doesn't mean "unable to perform." God is not impotent. He will do what He says He will do. The word *slow* is best translated differently.

Patient.

Nahum **says** God is patient in His anger. He gives people a chance to make things right. The results of this patience are staggering.

In the previous chapter, I created a scenario in which a creepy, older man seduced your teenage daughter. Let's revisit that story and imagine a response other than anger and jealousy. Imagine that your response was one of patience. Imagine knowing that this man was with your daughter, hurting your daughter, taking advantage of your daughter, in another country, far away from you. Imagine having the resources to deal with the situation, but instead, choosing to give the man multiple warnings.

What could possibly motivate this type of patience?

Only love.

You would have to possess such a deep love for this man that you would allow your daughter to suffer while he was given an opportunity **to** change his ways. God's patience is so great that He allows innocent people to suffer in order to give the monsters another chance.

The response to this patience is very different for the victim and the monster. If you are a victim, God's patience requires great faith on your part. One of Nahum's audiences, the oppressed Jewish people, needed to know that God was aware of their situation, yet patient in His anger.

If you are a monster, God's patience requires grateful repentance. When Jonah gave the Assyrians forty days to repent, they did so quickly and with gratefulness to God for suspending their judgment.

The question is, are you a victim or a monster?

The answer, of course, is both.

We are all victims.

We are all monsters.

Paul says in Romans that each of us has compiled a "long and sorry record of sin." We all have the monster DNA inside, and it is never far from making an appearance.

In American culture, no one struggles to be the victim. Our problem is that most of cannot see the monster inside of us. Until we see ourselves as both victim and monster, we will not be able to appreciate God's patient anger.

> You have been a victim. People have hurt you, betrayed you, lied about you, and abandoned you. When you see these people, you wonder why God hasn't dealt with them. After all, you are a Jesus follower, and it would be nice of God to come to your defense. You hope these people get what they deserve.

> You have been a monster. You have hurt, betrayed, lied about, and abandoned people. When you see these people, you thank God that He hasn't dealt with you. After all, you are a Jesus follower, and it would be just of God to deal with you quickly. You hope you don't get what you deserve.

Once we begin to see ourselves as victims and monsters, we will be able to respond appropriately to God's patient anger. We will have faith in God's loving promise and gratitude for God's loving patience.

CHAPTER 5:
Asking the Right Questions

A prominent evangelical came out recently with a shocking announcement about the devastating earthquake in Haiti. The earthquake was God's way of judging the Haitian people. Apparently the devil worship from past generations caused God to "open up a can" on the whole country.

The youth pastor in me wants to toilet paper his house, but I understand where he gets his ideas.

> "His way is in the whirlwind and the storm,
>> And clouds are the dust of His feet.
> He rebukes the sea and dries it up;
>> He makes all the rivers run dry.
> Bashan and Carmel wither
>> And the blossoms of Lebanon fade.
> The mountains quake before Him
>> And the hills melt away." **Nahum 1:3-4**

The First Testament is full of references to God's use of His good creation to judge evil. Because of these references, people like our prominent evangelical friend come to their conclusions. Does God use suffering like cancer or natural events like earthquakes to punish people or nations today?

I have absolutely no idea.

Before you try to get your money back, there are some things that I do know. My hope is that this chapter might move us toward a better understanding of God as the Comforting Avenger.

We should start by reminding ourselves of God's absolute perfection as judge. As we discussed in chapter 3, God is the only one capable of administering justice and taking out vengeance in perfect love. Because He is God, vengeance belongs to Him alone.

However, God not only bears responsibility for the act of vengeance; He bears responsibility for deciding which people will receive His vengeance. God determines how, when, and why He judges. This fact should bring the people of God to a logical conclusion concerning judgment.

We should be silent.

When we choose to speak God's judgment on a person or a nation in light of current events, we place ourselves in a role reserved for God alone. God knows what He is doing, and we do not. In the Biblical story of Job, God allowed destruction to be brought upon a person who had done nothing to deserve punishment. From the outside, Job's friends could only assume that his suffering was God's punishment . However, the beginning of the story tells us that sin did not cause Job's suffering. Job's friends thought they were right, but in reality they had no idea what God was up to.

In John 9, Jesus had an interesting conversation on the way we judge.

> "Walking down the street, Jesus saw a man blind from birth. His disciples asked, 'Rabbi, who sinned: this man or his parents, causing him to be born blind?' Jesus said, 'You're asking the wrong question. You're looking for someone to blame. There is no such cause-effect here. Look instead for what God can do. We need to be energetically at work for the One who sent me here, working while the sun shines. When night falls, the workday is over. For as long as I am in the world, there is plenty of light. I am the world's light.'"
> **John 9: 1-5 (Message)**

The disciples assumed that the pain in this situation was caused by generational sin, much like our prominent evangelical leader assumed that Haiti's problems were caused by generational sin. I love Jesus' response:

"You're asking the wrong question."

Jesus doesn't ever say that neither parent sinned. He simply says that the question isn't important. In the case of Nahum, God says the suffering is caused by sin. In the case of Job, God says the suffering has nothing to do with sin. In the case of the prominent evangelical, God is completely silent and the man just makes things up.

Whenever we try to determine the cause and effect for the judgment of others, we are playing way out of our league. Did God judge Haiti with an earthquake? I don't believe so, but I have to admit that I don't know. To say anything else is to take as my own the vengeance that belongs to God.

In John 9, Jesus replaces the wrong question the disciples ask with a better one:

"What can God do?"

What can God do in the face of this disaster? How can I help? Instead of seeking to explain why the suffering has happened, we must take the words of Jesus and be "energetically at work" for the restorative mission of God in the world. Service is our main responsibility when disaster or suffering has affected other people.

Sometimes, though, the disaster or suffering comes not to another person but to us. When faced with these situations, we must evaluate ourselves. The psalmist prayed that God would "search him and know his heart." This prayer models how we might evaluate personal disaster or suffering. When we suffer, we should allow the Spirit to examine our hearts for any sin or rebellion. Doing this does not mean that personal suffering is always caused by sin or rebellion. In fact, the point of self-evaluation is not only to determine the cause of our pain, but to maintain a right standing with God. In the words of C.S. Lewis, "Pain is God's megaphone."

The prominent evangelical had a good idea that was horribly applied. The process of determining the reason and passing judgment would have been fine had he been dealing with himself. To use Lewis's analogy, instead of allowing God to speak into his own life, the prominent evangelical took the megaphone out of God's hands and proceeded to scream at the poorest nation on the planet.

Please do not hear me saying that God does not judge sin. Scripture is clear that, in the end, God's judgment will be swift and terrible. From a human perspective, we easily forget that God doesn't need a "hands-on" approach to be in complete control of the world. In other words, God can let events develop naturally over time, while still controlling their outcome. This reality led David to say,

> "This is too much, too wonderful, I can't take it all in."
> **Psalm 139:6**

When suffering and disaster come to others, we serve.

When suffering and disaster come to us, we evaluate our hearts with the guidance of the Spirit.

In all suffering and disaster, we place our faith in the perfect love and judgment of the Comforting Avenger.

CHAPTER 6:
God is Good?

"The LORD is good, a refuge in times of trouble.

He cares for those who trust in him." **Nahum 1:7**

If you know a verse from Nahum, it is probably the one you just read. It's the kind of verse that makes Christians hold their heads high and write really good worship tunes.

Speaking of worship tunes, the church I went to in the 90's used to sing this one:

God is good, all the time.
He put a song of praise in this heart of mine.
God is good, all the time.
Through the darkest night, His light will shine.
God is good, God is good, all the time.

We sang this song with big smiles and a lot of hand clapping. God is good all the time, and if you don't believe us, just read Nahum 1:7!

But don't read verse six:

"Who can withstand His indignation?

Who can endure His fierce anger?
His wrath is poured out like fire;

The rocks are shattered before Him." **Nahum 1:6**

Or verse eight:

"But with an overwhelming flood

He will make an end of Nineveh;
He will pursue his foes into darkness." **Nahum 1:8**

In fact, of the forty-seven verses that make up God's vision to Nahum, only three speak of anything we would consider good. The other ninety-four percent of the book addresses topics such as God's use of evil empires to destroy other evil empires, the death of innocent children, and the death of God's enemies.

Try clapping your hands to that.

Before we go on, let me confess. I believe with everything in me that God is absolutely good, both His nature and His actions. I also believe that God's goodness is His most misunderstood attribute. In this chapter I will try to help you understand what makes God good.

As I mentioned earlier, we have a nasty habit of making God into a really powerful human. We believe that God should think and decide in the same way the best of humanity would think and decide. When God does not act like a noble human, we often question His goodness.

Job struggles with God's goodness. As strange as it seems, the story indicates that God allows Satan to take Job's stuff and kill Job's children so that God can prove a point about the faithfulness of Job. The Bible says that Job was "blameless and upright," but somehow he was placed in the crossfire between God and Satan.

Throughout the book, Job honestly expresses his frustration with God. Listen to Job at the height of his frustration:

"I'm not letting up--I'm standing my ground. My complaint is legitimate. God has no right to treat me like this--it isn't fair! If I knew where on earth to find Him, I'd go straight to Him, I'd lay my case before Him face-to-face; give Him all my arguments first hand. I'd find out exactly what He's thinking, discover what's going on in His head. Do you think He'd dismiss me or bully me?"
Job 23:1-6 (Message)

Job seems to have a real problem with the way God is handling his situation. is a good guy getting a bad deal, and God had better get on the ball. Eventually, God answers Job, but not in the way you might expect.

"And now, finally, God answered Job from the eye of a violent storm. He said: 'Why do you confuse the issue? Why do you talk without knowing what you're talking about?'"
Job 38:1-2 (Message)

God asks Job a series of sarcastic rhetorical questions. Has he ever created anything? Has he ever told the morning to get started? Where was he when God created the world? Has Job ever taught a lion how to hunt?

Why does God ask Job these questions? What does God want Job to understand? God wants Job to know that they are not alike. Yes, Job is made in God's image, but Job is not God. There is significant space between the two of them.

After God has finished, Job has an opportunity to respond. I think he understood God's message:

"I'm speechless, in awe--words fail me. I never should have opened my mouth. I've talked too much, way too much. I'm ready to shut up and listen. I'm convinced: You can do anything and everything. Nothing and no one can upset Your plans. You asked, 'Who is this muddying the water, ignorantly confusing the issue, second guessing My purposes?' I admit it. I was the one. I babbled on about things far beyond me, made small talk about wonders way over my head." **Job 40:3-5;42:1,3 (Message)**

To see God as good, we first must see Him as God.

Seeing him as God means we cannot measure God's goodness against human experience or human goodness. In our two-dimensional view, goodness requires all evil to be out of sight. God is not two-dimensional; instead you might think of Him as omni-dimensional. God's goodness is neither tame nor domesticated, but a powerful goodness that brings justice into the world. God doesn't play by our rules. If He did, you really wouldn't want Him as a God.

In Nahum, God was willing to take responsibility for the judgment of the wicked and the protection of the innocent. He was willing to intervene in human history, transcend the limits of human goodness, and guarantee perfect justice for all. No human could ever claim that responsibility and still be called good.

"'For My thoughts are not your thoughts, neither are your ways My ways,' declares the Lord. 'As the heavens are higher than the earth, so are My ways higher than your ways and My thoughts than your thoughts.'" **Isaiah 55:8-9**

So how do we live with a picture of a God that is good in everything He does?

Faith.

We must cultivate a faith that believes in the real version of God, not the human one. This faith requires absolute trust in the goodness of God. Too many of us carry a faith in the human god that quickly falls apart in times of suffering or despair.

> Faith in the human god is enough when you're having a bad day,
>> but it's not enough when your spouse dies.

> Faith in the human god is enough when your kid shows attitude,
>> but it's not enough when your daughter runs away.

> Faith in the human god is enough when you're short on cash,
>> but it's not enough when you lose your job.

Faith in the real version of God means that we trust His goodness in verses six and eight just as much as we do in verse seven. This faith asks us to believe that if we lost everything we have tomorrow, God would still be completely good.

Look at this verse one more time:

> "The LORD is good, a refuge in times of trouble.
>> He cares for those who trust in him." **Nahum 1:7**

Nahum teaches us this: if your trust is in God, He will care for you. If in your darkest moment, you hold on to the goodness of the real version of God, He will become your refuge. You will make it through to the other side.

> "The LORD gave and the LORD has taken away;
> May the name of the LORD be praised." **Job 1:21**

CHAPTER 7:
Bad Conclusions

In teaching a book like Nahum, I fear that people will draw bad conclusions about how to handle our enemies. Let's face it: Christians get excited at the prospect of a good fight. Before you know it, they've turned Israel into Apollo Creed, Assyria into Ivan Drago, and God into Rocky Balboa.

My fear is compounded because I live in Michigan. I love Michigan. I even own a t-shirt that says, "Smitten with the Mitten." But some in our state get a bit drunk on the crazy juice sometimes, enough to get us in the news a few times each year. Here are the 2010 submissions so far:

Hutaree, a Michigan militia group based twenty minutes from my house, describe themselves as "Christian soldiers preparing for the arrival of and battle with the anti-Christ." Recently, the Department of Homeland Security joined with the Joint Terrorism Task Force to make several arrests.

Trijicon, a precision gun-sight company with multi-year contracts with the military, is headquartered in Michigan. They are a Christian company, so naturally they decided to inscribe Bible verses on the gun sights. The guns are currently being used in Iraq and Afghanistan.

An older man I know proudly wears a t-shirt that reads, "Pray for President Obama – Psalm 109:8." That particular verse says, "May his days be few, may another take his place of leadership." The next verse says, "May his children be fatherless and his wife a widow. May his children be wandering beggars."

It was the man in the t-shirt that prompted me to send this message on Twitter:

"If you're already crazy, the Bible will just make things worse."

The Bible becomes dangerous when well-intentioned people twist it to say things they think are important. In order to honor scripture, we must refuse to manipulate it for our purposes. This means paying attention to context, historical interpretation, and the counsel of our Christian community. With these cautions in mind, let's look at some ways Nahum is commonly twisted.

God's anger in Nahum is sometimes used as a parenting strategy, used by parents to defend what I call "angry parenting." Some of us parents yell, threaten, manipulate, and judge, all in the name of Biblical discipline. We become confused, seeing our role with our kids as God, not parent. The result is that our kids become confused as well. They start to see God's anger as less than perfect, kind of like Mom's anger when she has had a really long day and loses her cool.

God's anger in Nahum is a response to the evil actions of the Assyrians. He responds to the pain of the helpless. This is a far cry from the anger that most of us feel toward our kids.

If we're honest, most of our anger towards our kids is sinful and in opposition to God. In case you think I'm getting a little "preachy" here:

> I'm a pastor (professional Christian) and the parent of two amazing kids. I'm amazed at how quickly I can manipulate Scripture and justify my irritation and anger as "good parenting." When I become angry with my kids for fighting or talking back, it is very rarely because I want them to understand my love and ambition for their spiritual development. I get angry because I am tired, busy, or sick of dealing with them.

When I'm at my best as a parent, I am not angry. This doesn't mean that I don't discipline consistently or speak firmly. It simply means that I see my role as parent and not as God. My children don't need another version of God; they need a better version of parent. They need to be nurtured, loved, heard, coached, and taught the way of Jesus. None of these things can be done in anger.

Nahum's words against Assyria are sometimes used to justify war against the enemies of America. We see ourselves as Israel, our enemies as Assyria. We play the role of Nahum, announcing God's judgment on our enemies because of their actions against us. This is an error of interpretation for several reasons.

First, God's allegiance lies with Himself, not with America. God is not loyal to America; He is loyal to His perfect justice. As hard as it is for patriots to hear, God has not given us a special place above other nations. He doesn't have a picture of Lee Greenwood on His wall. We twist Scripture when we see America as God's chosen people.

Second, God judged Assyria's cruelty and violence so that Israel could be rescued. As Americans, we are not suffering due to military oppression. We have certainly been hurt in the past, but we are not actively suffering now. God will not rise up against our enemies to relieve us from a situation that does not exist.

Third, the violence in Nahum was one-sided. Assyria was facing no resistance as they destroyed the world. If God were to intervene in our American conflicts in order to stop the suffering of innocents, can we be sure that He would stand with us?

I love America, and I am grateful for my freedom. I have friends in our military who I love very much. My caution is that we must not make God American or make our wars extensions of God's justice.

God's anger in Nahum is sometimes used by American Christians to condemn America. In this case, Christians play the role of God by loudly proclaiming judgment on America for any number of things:

> Homosexuality
> Health care
> Abortion
> Democrats
> Lady Gaga

You might have seen Christian groups with hateful signs towards homosexuals or graphic posters displaying aborted fetuses. You might have been forced to watch a Lady Gaga music video. While the above things are not equal, the list is not really the problem. The problem is how to respond.

You might be expecting me to say that Christians should steer clear of involvement in these tough issues. Nothing could be further from the truth. As long as we are loving and respectful (a tall order for some), Christians have a right to be involved in issues. When we confuse involvement and judgment, we twist the message of Nahum.

As we discussed in chapter five, we are not responsible to decide how, when, or why God judges people. The list above is an intentional mix of issues on which the Bible speaks and issues on which the Bible is silent. I made it that way to underscore my point that judgment always belongs to God. The issues we're facing will never change that fact.

The Bible is a dangerous book, and bad interpretations have hurt many people. As we allow the Spirit to guide our lives, we should ask ourselves if we are misusing scripture in any way. The Bible works best when we allow it to say what it says, and not what we want it to say.

Questions for Further Reflection

1. What characteristics of God have you found to be confusing? What have you thought or read about God that made you angry? Are there parts of the Bible that you have skipped over because they didn't make sense? If you came across a particularly hard part of the Bible, whom would you talk to about it? Why?

2. What do you think matters to God? What do you think makes Him angry? What kind of behavior does He refuse to tolerate? How do you think God responds to these situations? What has brought you to these conclusions?

3. In what ways can you resonate with Nahum's story? In what ways do you feel oppression? Do you ever feel like your running from the bully? Has there been a time when you felt God's presence standing in your defense?

4. What would you identify as the big monsters in our world today? What would you identify as the big monsters in your life right now? After reading about the violence of the Assyrians, do you feel differently about the way God punished them? Does the fact that God had given Assyria a second chance change the way you feel about their punishment? What are some of the ways that we "revoke our repentance"? In what areas are you tempted to take God lightly?

5. Make a playful list of some of the bad versions of God you have adopted. What circumstances have caused you to adopt these versions of God? In your own words, write a definition of God's jealousy. Do you find God's jealousy hard to accept? Why? Can you think of a time when you have chose forgiveness over vengeance? What was the outcome?

6. How do you feel about the concept of God's patience? If love is the motivation for God's patience, what is the motivation for his judgment and his anger? What are the potential ways that we might play the role of victim? What are the ways that we are playing monster? How does our understanding of patience change depending on our role? Do you think people can play both roles simultaneously?How have you felt previously about people linking disasters or current events with God's judgment? Do you believe that God uses disasters to judge people? Why or why not? Are you comfortable with taking Ben's, "I don't know" mentality?

7. If someone asked you to defend God's goodness, how would you answer? In what ways do you see humans holding God to their standards? Have you ever felt like Job felt when he questioned God? In your own words, write out what you would say to God if you could speak to him concerning your darkest moment.

8. Make your own list of bad conclusions that people might draw from the book of Nahum? Which item from that list is most tempting to you? Do you ever find yourself thinking that God is American? Where does this thinking come from?

The Elements of Spiritual Formation

Something For Your Soul
SO, WHAT DO YOU KNOW…

Consider what you know about God. If you were to describe God, what words would you use? What formed you ideas of God?

How does the idea of Comforting Avenger challenge, change or add to your existing perspective? What does this mean for how you live your life?

We encourage you to spend some time praying about your ideas and perspectives on God. Ask God to help you establish a solid and healthy view of who He is and His role in your life. Be a careful listener.

Something For Your Relationships
BULLY UP…

We invite you to hold a microscope over your relationships for a second. What do you see? Bully or bullied? Maybe a little of both? Either way, owning up to the truth is not easy. It is, however, necessary.

As Jesus Followers, we are called to be carriers of hope, not intimidation. How are you at being a dispenser of hope? Could you do better (i.e. be slower to judge, use uplifting words, sacrifice some time to give to another)? Ask God to reveal ways you could speak and carry hope into the lives of others.

Something For Your Church
CONTEXT MATTERS…

How we speak about God, the church and others simply matters. Too often we open our mouths without knowing the full story, Scripture included. This does nothing to help the view of the Church in the eyes of the world.

We encourage you to check out the story. Read the context surrounding the verse(s) in which you have interest. Invite others into the conversation. Pray about what you're learning and remain humble in your opinions.

Something For Your World
THE RIGHT THING…

Take a look at what the Bible says in James 4.16-17 (The Message):

> "As it is, you are full of your grandiose selves. All such vaunting self-importance is evil. In fact, if you know the right thing to do and don't do it, that, for you, is evil."

Do you ever find your heart nudging you to act, to make a difference, but yet you fail to follow through? If so, what holds you back?

Make an action plan. Begin with prayer. Ask God to forgive you for falling short of acting in the past. Find something or someone that peaks your passion and look for ways you can make a difference, no matter how small. Give yourself a deadline for acting. If necessary, invite someone to hold you accountable.

the comfort of vengeance

SECTION TWO
Nahum 1:15-2:13

Nahum Chapter Two:
The Cobblestone Translation

Your enemy is coming to crush you, Nineveh.
Man the fort!
Watch the road!
Dress for battle!
Call out your forces!

Destroyers have destroyed God's people and ruined their vines,
But the Lord will restore the honor of Jacob.

Shields flash red in the sunlight;
The warriors are clad in scarlet.
Watch as their glittering chariots move into position;
A spiked forest of brandished spears.

The chariots race madly through the streets,
And rush wildly through the squares.
They look like torches; they run like lightning.

The Assyrian king rallies his men,
        But they stumble on the way.
They dash to the city wall,
        And the defense is prepared.
The river gates are thrown open,
        And the palace is destroyed.

Nineveh's exile has been decreed.
        The slave girls moan like doves and beat their breasts,
            Because they are sad.

Nineveh is like a pool, and its water is draining away.
        "Stop! Stop!" they cry, but no one turns back.

Take the silver! Take the gold!
        There's no end to Nineveh's treasures.

Nineveh is robbed, ruined, and destroyed.
        Hearts sink,
            Knees fold,
                Stomachs retch,
                    And every face grows pale.

Where is the famous and fierce Assyrian lion,
        And the place where they feed their young?
It was a place where people _ like lions and their cubs _
        Walked freely and without fear.

The lion tore in pieces enough for his cubs,
          Killed for his lionesses, filling his lairs with the kill
    And his dens with the prey.

    "See, I am your enemy," says the Lord of Heaven's armies.
        "I will burn up your chariots in smoke,
And the sword will kill your young lions.
        Never again will your plunder conquered nations,
And the voice of your messengers shall be heard no more."

CHAPTER 8:
The Restoration Movement

"Look, there on the mountains,
    The feet of one who brings good news,
Who proclaims peace! Celebrate your festivals,
    Oh Judah, and fulfill your vows." **Nahum 1:15**

"The LORD will restore the splendor of Jacob
    Like the splendor of Israel,
Though destroyers have laid them to waste
    And have ruined their vines." **Nahum 2:2**

In 2006 I spent some time in New Orleans, rebuilding homes after hurricane Katrina. Early on, I found myself right on the ocean at an oyster farm that had been destroyed by the hurricane. The first people I met were the farm's owners, Bubba and Momma.

Bubba's and Momma's lives were wrapped up in that farm, and now it was gone. They literally had nothing left. My job was to help clear the property for rebuilding. If you have never seen a hurricane site, then you have no idea what "clearing the property" means. Everything was broken; everything stank, and everything weighed a ton.

In our third day of moving rubble, we were bringing down the remains of a barn. Pulling down the only standing wall, we came face to face with three giant sunflowers.

This might seem like nothing, but you must remember that there was nothing left. The trees, buildings, and houses were gone. Three giant sunflowers, however, were standing tall. In the middle of devastation had emerged a sign of restoration.

Our team held onto those sunflowers during the long, hot days. Those three plants reminded us that God was not finished; in fact, He was beginning again. I believe that God is the founder of the world's largest restoration movement. He is continually healing and restoring what is broken in this world.

Nahum 1:15 is one of four verses in the entire book meant to bring hope to the victims in Israel. Nahum describes the "feet of the one who brings good news," specifically the good news of rescue from the Assyrians. Nahum borrowed this phrase from Isaiah:

> "How beautiful on the mountains are the feet of those who bring good news, who proclaim peace." **Isaiah 52:7**

About six hundred years later, Paul borrowed the phrase again:

> "For everyone who calls on the name of the Lord will be saved. How, then, can they call on the one they have not believed in? And how can they believe in the one of whom they have not heard? And how can they hear without someone preaching to them? And how can they preach unless they are sent? As it is written, 'How beautiful are the feet of those who bring good news!'" **Romans 10:13-15**

Paul used the phrase at the end of a series of questions for the church, encouraging them to spread the good news (hope and peace) of God found through Jesus.

Notice the progression as this phrase is repeated. Isaiah spoke of a message of peace during war. Nahum spoke of a message of hope during oppression. Paul spoke of a message of the peace and hope found in Jesus.

Paul used First Testament language to say, "You are the messenger now."

God is restoring the world, and we are commissioned to join Him in that movement. At Westwinds, we like to say it this way:

We shadow God as He heals the world.

We are made in God's image—shadows, if you will. As God carries out His restoration movement, He invites us to be a part of putting things back together. He wants to grow us up—like the giant sunflowers—in the middle of our broken world, as signs of life for everyone. Let's examine a couple of areas in which we are able to join His restoration movement.

God invites us to join Him in the restoration of people. Nahum's message to Israel offers hope through restoration:

"Now I will break their yoke from your neck,
and tear your shackles away." **Nahum 1:13**

God wanted Israel to know that He loved them and was going to change their situation. According to Paul, God wants to use us to accomplish this same kind of change in our world today. As followers of Jesus, restored through the cross, we shadow God by sharing this hope.

It is important to understand our responsibility here. We are to share the good news of hope in Jesus so that people can be restored. Nowhere are we told to beat people with the rules of religion. Too often our efforts to share the gospel begin with the rules instead of the message of hope, making the good news feel more like driver's training than the restoration of the world through Jesus.

How do we share the good news of hope in Jesus? We love. We find ways to invest in the lives of others, offering a picture of the hope Jesus brings.

"We loved you so much that we shared not only the gospel with you, but our very lives as well because you were so dear to us."
1 Thessalonians 2:8 (NLT)

Another way we might join God in the restoration of people is through social justice. Millions of people around the world are suffering in slavery and poverty. Most of us have the resources to make a difference, but we lack the motivation and education to join the movement. Shadowing God in the restoration of people will require you to learn the issues and take real steps to help.

God also invites us to join Him in the restoration of creation. Nahum 2:2 is another of the hopeful verses for God's people. In this verse, God makes a curious statement that at first glance seems like a throwaway. Acknowledging that the Assyrians have ruined Israel's vines, in His message about restoration, God makes sure he mentions the plants.

The Assyrians were famous for their total destruction of the nations they conquered. After taking everything they wanted, they always burned the entire area: trees, bushes, animals, everything. One historian compared the Assyrian burnings to Stalin's "scorched earth." In light of this practice, God's bringing up the vines is certainly not a coincidence.

We have discussed God's restoration of people, but we must be sure not to miss the complete picture. The Bible repeatedly states that God loves all of His creation.

"The Lord is good to all; He has compassion on all He has made."
Psalm 145:9

"And you must keep my decrees and my laws…and if you defile the land, it will vomit you out as it vomited out the nations that were before you." **Leviticus 18:26, 28**

"Don't desecrate the land in which you live. I live here, too—I, God, live in the same neighborhood." **Numbers 35:34 (Message)**

A more theologically accurate statement would be this: God wants to restore His creation, including the people. While the church at large is making strides in creation care, Christians have largely overlooked God's love for all things. A guy I follow on Twitter said this recently:

"Happy Earth Day! Or, as conservative Evangelicals call it, Thursday."

God cares deeply about His creation, and as his shadows, we need to care as well. This means we have to change our lifestyles to reflect creation restoration. I admit that I did not grow up caring about any of these things. Fortunately, I have friends like Corey and Kendall who are educating me. Corey and Kendall have put in the time to understand the issues threatening our planet/God's creation. They make conscious choices to ensure that they are shadowing God well. If, like me, you are ignorant about recycling, food sources, pollution, and global warming; you should investigate these issues that are clearly important to God.

God is restoring the whole world, and He wants you to shadow Him. This process will require some sacrifice, but in the end you will be a part of God's redemptive story.

What could be more beautiful?

CHAPTER 9:
Stories of Hope

Liz Murray has an inspirational story.

She was born in the Bronx, New York, to poor, drug-addicted, HIV-infected parents. At age 9, Liz lived in a filthy apartment with her sister and drug-addicted parents. She spent her tip money from bagging groceries on food for the family, usually eating that food on the same table her parents used to snort cocaine. Food and cocaine: not the best combination.

When Liz was 16, her mother died of AIDS, her father moved to a homeless shelter, and Liz found herself alone. She barely went to school and spent her nights sleeping on park benches, subways, or a friend's parents' couch.

Liz's life turned around when she met Dale, the principal at Humanities Preparatory Academy in Chelsea, Manhattan. Dale agreed to tutor her before and after school if she was willing to do the work. Although she was homeless and caring for her younger sister, Liz graduated in only two years. She was awarded a *New York Times* scholarship for needy students and accepted into Harvard University. She eventually graduated from Harvard with a bachelor's degree in psychology. Last year she began taking graduate classes at Harvard, in hopes of earning a doctorate in clinical psychology to counsel people from all walks of life.

Liz's story was made into a movie called, *Homeless to Harvard.* Now she travels around the country, telling her story and helping young people. Last year when I had the chance to hear Liz speak, I was completely inspired. As she spoke of the one person who never gave up on her, I was inspired to be more faithful to the students at Student Journey. When she talked about her perseverance in the face of adversity, I was determined never to give up.

Stories inspire us. They give us new dreams, new possibilities, and new hope. When we feel as if we can't go on, sometimes a good story is exactly what we need. When kids affected by poverty hear Liz speak, they start to believe that maybe they have an alternate future. Liz's story gives them hope.

When Israel found themselves being tormented by the Assyrians with no hope of escape, they turned to stories for their comfort. As they felt the cruelty of the Assyrian people, they would recount the stories of God's faithfulness in Egypt. Remembering the story of God's rescuing their ancestors from a wicked nation gave them courage to hang on.

When reading Nahum, you might wonder why he felt the need to go into such graphic detail regarding the destruction of Nineveh. Look at the detail Nahum used:

> "The chariots pour into the streets.
> They fill the public squares,
> flaming like torches in the sun,
> like lighting darting and flashing.
> The Assyrian king rallies his men,
> but they stagger and stumble." **Nahum 2:4-5**

Nahum might have been specific so that history would validate the power of God, but I think he had a more practical reason. He knew the power his story could have in generations to come. Nahum was specific so that any time God's people were suffering, they could remember that God was still fighting for them.

Soon after the time of Nahum, Israel was defeated and destroyed by the Babylonian Empire. The Babylonians took the Israelites as slaves and destroyed their cities. For almost one hundred years, the Israelites suffered. How did they keep from giving up?

> They told Nahum's story, and they remembered that God was with them.

Seven hundred years later, the descendants of the exiled Jewish people were suffering again. Jesus had risen and ascended; the Christian church was just starting, and the persecution of Jewish Christians by both Romans and other Jews was widespread. Followers of Jesus were being tortured and murdered for their belief. How did these early Christians stay hopeful?

> They told Nahum's story, and they remembered that God was with them.

Eighteen hundred years later, the Jewish descendants of those early Christians found themselves being hunted by Hitler. Six million Jews were killed over a six-year period. Those who survived were never the same. How did these suffering Jews stay strong in the face of such brutality?

> They told Nahum's story, and they remembered that God was with them.

In America we need a different kind of hope. Our marriages are suffering; our jobs are not secure, and our families are destabilized. In my city of Jackson, Michigan, there used to be a billboard that read, "Last one out of Jackson turn off the lights." We are in need of hope, and we are in need of stories.

We need to find the stories that help us stay hopeful in the face of life's hardships. As Christians we need to know the stories in Scripture that show us the promises of God through Jesus. See how Paul told the story of Jesus to the church in Rome:

"You see, at just the right time, when we were still powerless, Christ died for the ungodly. Very rarely will anyone die for a righteous man, though for a good man someone might possibly dare to die. But God demonstrates His own love for us in this: While we were still sinners, Christ died for us." **Romans 5:6-8**

Paul also used his own story in his letter to the church in Galatia:

"You know what I was like when I followed the Jewish religion--how I violently persecuted the Christians. I did my best to get rid of them. I was one of the most religious Jews of my own age, and I tried as hard as possible to follow all the old traditions of my religion. Then something happened! For it pleased God in his kindness to choose me and call me, even before I was born! What undeserved mercy!" **Galatians 1:13-15 (NLT)**

Nahum's story provided hope to Israel because the people never stopped telling it. If we are going to gain hope from the stories of our faith in Jesus, we have to tell them in our churches, to our children, with our spouses. These stories must be part of who we are.

We need not only the stories from Scripture, but new stories as well. One thing I love about Westwinds is that we are a storytelling church. We use every excuse imaginable to capture people's stories on video, over lunch, or on Twitter. We do this because we know that stories create stories. We see it at Westwinds every time we have a baptism.

Our last baptism was on Easter Sunday. We heard stories of hope and Jesus and rescue from so many people. At the end of the service, we invited people who were considering baptism to grab a small vial and fill it with water from the baptismal hot tub. This vial would serve as a sign of their desire to be baptized. I stood off to the side of the hot tub in tears, watching a stream of people fill their vials. These people had been inspired by the stories of God alive in others, and now a new story was being told.

What are your stories? Where has God been present in your history? When has God proven himself to be fighting for you?

In the First Testament, God's people built altars as a way of marking the movement of God on their behalf. I love this concept, and I have several "altars" around my office.

> I have a British pound on my bookshelf, from the time we worked with refugees in London. That coin reminds me of how God showed up in ways I didn't think were possible.

> I have a weird Jamaican plaque on my other bookshelf. That plaque reminds me of how God rescued two of my students.

> On my desk at Westwinds, I have the Bible that my dad bought for my mom before she died. It reminds me of how God sustained our family through the darkest hours.

Maybe as you read these words, you feel short on hope. Your finances are bad; your job is gone; your family is shaky, and you don't see an end in sight. Maybe you need to revisit some old stories, create a new story, build some altars. My prayer for you is that in the process of remembering, you will find that God has been with you the whole time.

CHAPTER 10:
Riches to Rags

Have you ever fantasized about winning the lottery? I think everyone has made an imaginary list to itemize how he would spend the ten million dollar jackpot.

> Purchase of an entire Best Buy store
> Purchase of every Apple product ever made
> A sports car for every day of the week
> The factory where Skittles are made
> A butler named "Winston"

That is, of course, my wife's list. My list is mostly charitable giving and college money for my kids.

The Assyrians did not need to fantasize about wealth; they truly had it all. Because of their aggressive military tactics, the Assyrian empire had taken the resources of almost every other nation in the world. Nahum described the Assyrian wealth as *endless*.

Even more interesting is that the Assyrians did not need the wealth to fund their conquests. Because they controlled the world, they could literally take whatever they wanted from almost anyone. The Assyrians amassed incredible wealth simply because they could, with the result that they literally had more stuff than they could store. In fact, most of their slaves were put to work building new temples that served as very fancy storage units. In chapter two, Nahum makes reference to the Assyrian wealth.

> "Nineveh is like a pool, and its water is draining away.
> 'Stop! Stop!' they cry, but no one turns them back.
> Plunder the silver! Plunder the gold! The supply is endless,
>   the wealth from all its treasures." **Nahum 2:8-9**

The popular interpretation of this passage is that serves as a warning to the wealthy. Assyria was the richest nation in the world, but God took away their riches. When we look more carefully, however, I believe we can come to a different conclusion. God most definitely judged the Assyrians for the wealth they had, but not simply for having it. The Assyrians were judged for leaving God out of the equation.

The Assyrians left God out of the equation when they killed people in order to take their possessions and when they refused to put any restrictions on the way they used their wealth. Because of this behavior, part of their judgment was the loss of their treasures.

Nahum described Assyrian money as a pool whose water is draining. This was a direct reference to the system of levies built by King Sennacherib. The levies allowed Nineveh to have water flowing into and out of the city. When the Babylonians and Medes captured Nineveh, one of their crucial moves was to gain control of the levies. Nahum was saying that eventually the Assyrians' wealth would slip through their fingers like water through a drain, and they wouldn't be able to stop it. Not because they were wealthy, but because they left God out of the equation. They refused to pay attention to God in regards to their money.

I just wish this chapter had some relevance today.

There is a very popular notion that America will be judged for its great wealth, but I don't believe that notion to be true. I believe the application for us is the same as it was for the Assyrians. We aren't practicing any moderation, just as we aren't paying attention to God. Take a moment to think about the similarities between Assyria and America when it comes to money.

Assyria was the richest nation in the world.

Assyria was forced to build extra buildings to hold their possessions.

Almost everyone not in military or royalty was employed in the management of goods.

The kings and the wealthy lived in segmented parts of the country, subtly separated from the poor.

There are definitely similarities between the wealth of Assyria and America; the response is not to condemn wealth. Instead, our prosperity should lead us to evaluation.

When it comes to wealth, am I leaving God out of the equation?

In order to evaluate how God fits into our money, we need to hear His thoughts on the subject.

"If I get hungry, do you think I'd tell you? All creation and its bounty are mine." **Psalm 50:10 (Message)**

In this verse, we see that God's motivation to be part of the equation is not simply to get a cut. God is not Tony Soprano, carefully and discreetly managing His associates. He is the creator and owner of all things, including what He has given to us. This leads us to believe that God has another motive for wanting to be involved in our wealth.

"Do not store up for yourselves treasures on earth, where moth and rust destroy, and where thieves break in and steal. But store up for yourselves treasures in heaven, where moth and rust do not destroy, and where thieves do not break in and steal. For where your treasure is, there your heart will be also." **Matthew 6:19-21**

These words of Jesus reveal God's primary motivation for involvement in our finances. He wants us. From the beginning, God's wanted to be in a relationship with His creation. God wanted to be part of the equation in Assyria's wealth, but only because He wanted to be part of the equation in Assyria! God knows that if He is part of the equation where our wealth is concerned, He will be part of the equation in everything else.

So how do we make sure that God is part of the equation? Jesus told us not to store up treasure here on earth. In the Message Bible, Eugene Peterson translates the idea of storing up treasure as "hoarding." I would never introduce myself to you as a hoarder, but I'm more of a hoarder than I care to admit.

Hoarding happens when a person or a people continue to accumulate stuff beyond what they need to survive. But hoarding also implies the stranglehold we have on the things we accumulate, or the stranglehold they have on us. When accumulating more consumes us to the point of controlling our life, we become hoarders.

Jesus gave an alternate picture to the idea of hoarding. He told us to "store up treasure in heaven." When I was a kid, this concept made no sense to me. In fact, I thought the church must be heaven because they were always asking for our money. We can best understand Jesus' words through the concept of generosity. Luke records a slightly different version of Jesus' words than Matthew:

"Sell your possessions and give to the poor. Provide purses for yourselves that will not wear out, a treasure in heaven that will not be exhausted, where no thief comes near and no moth destroys. For where your treasure is, there your heart will be also."
Luke 12:33-34

Jesus defines storing up treasure in heaven as being generous to those who are in need. Instead of accumulating and guarding our possessions, we find ways to give them away. This action makes God part of the equation, because what we give away can never take His rightful place in our heart.

In his book Free of Charge, Miroslav Volf says that people are primarily takers, getters, and givers. Takers acquire wealth illegally or violently; getters acquire wealth legitimately, and givers distribute wealth generously. The Assyrians were most definitely takers. They brutalized children, murdered women, and destroyed cities in order to accumulate wealth. God wanted the Assyrians to become getters by acquiring wealth legitimately. Most of us, however, are already getters. We work very hard to acquire wealth through honest and legitimate means. God's goal is for us to become givers by distributing wealth generously.

At this point in any discussion about wealth, the practicality will cause people to be a bit uncomfortable. Some will claim that all Christians should be poor. Others will condemn the purchase of anything nice. Many people will feel guilty about the things they have. The tension is best summed up with a question that a teenager asked me recently while I was teaching on this subject:

"So you're saying I can't ever buy a new iPod?"

Each of us must listen to the Holy Spirit to determine how he uses his wealth, but one practice has helped me resolve this tension. I practice strategic generosity. In other words, before I buy my new iPod (inflow) I make sure that I am contributing to the movement of God through the church and in the world (outflow). Nineveh used their levy system strategically to control the inflow and outflow of water for the city. Making God part of the equation means that we are strategically generous. When we practice this action, we lay up treasures in heaven that cannot be destroyed.

Nahum told the Assyrians that because they had left God out of the equation, He was going to take their wealth away from them. Eventually this is what always happens. Even the richest person in the world can't take his money with him after life. We should be grateful to God for what He has given and strategically generous with what we give.

CHAPTER 11:
The Pursuit of Friendship

> I'm going to get rid of all my enemies.
> I will turn them into friends. **Abraham Lincoln**

I'm not sure how any of us survived before Facebook. In the 1990s BF (Before Facebook), I had no way of tracking my true number of friends. Thanks to Facebook, I now know that my exact number of friends is one thousand one hundred and thirteen.

It is funny how our social media has changed the concept of friendship to include someone I met at a conference last year, my fifth grade teacher, the guy who cut my hair when I lived in Minneapolis, and another guy named Ben Redmond. I would be tempted to disregard altogether this idea of friendship except for one thing.

God is also my Facebook friend.

Because I am one of God's three million Facebook friends, He and I swap pics and pokes like nobody's business. He hasn't clicked the "like" button on any of my statuses yet, but at least He didn't deny my friend request.

> "'I am against you,'
>> Declares the LORD Almighty.
> 'I will burn up your chariots in smoke,
>> And the sword will devour your young lions.
> I will leave you no prey on the earth.
>> The voices of your messengers
> Will no longer be heard.'" **Nahum 2:13**

Think for a moment about the weight of this verse. The all-powerful God of the world told the people of Nineveh that He stands against them. Not only are they not Facebook friends; they are enemies.

"When they heard the sound of God strolling in the garden in the evening breeze, the Man and his Wife hid in the trees of the garden, hid from God." **Genesis 3:8 (Message)**

God's desire from the beginning of creation was friendship. In Genesis we see an image of God walking through the garden, giving the idea that this walking was a normal occurrence. God wanted to be with His people. But as the story unfolds, we see Adam and Eve sin with devastating results. God kicks them out of the garden, and their relationship with Him is completely changed. God is no longer with His people.

In the case of the Assyrians, God sends Jonah to warn them of God's judgment. Jonah obeys at great personal risk. The people repent, and the last words of Jonah read,

"Should I not be concerned about that great city?" **Jonah 4:11**

But less than two hundred years later, God gives Nahum a message of inevitable judgment. The last words of Nahum read,

"Everyone who hears the news about you
    Claps his hands at your fall,
For who has not felt your endless cruelty?" **Nahum 3:19**

God is for the Assyrians as their friend in Jonah, but He is against the Assyrians as their enemy in Nahum.

This begs the question, "Is God for us or against us?" The answer is a resounding, "Yes!" God is both for us and against us. He is for us when we live in obedience to Him; He is against us when we rebel. This truth is very tough to hear but very important to understand. Friendship with God isn't like friendship on Facebook, or anywhere else, for that matter. It's not two parties giving equally, because we aren't even close to being equal parties. Friendship with God is an agreement between God and us that says we will both do things His way. In our human thinking this is the most selfish friendship imaginable, but as we have discussed already, God is not like us.

At the beginning of this chapter, I mentioned that God's desire from the start was friendship. If this premise is true, then why does He ever stand against us? God only stands against us in an effort to restore friendship. Said another way, God is only ever against us because He is ultimately for us. As the Comforting Avenger, God will stand against us if we violate the conditions of His friendship, but only so that friendship can be repaired.

God sent Jonah to Nineveh in an effort to restore friendship. Nineveh accepted for a while but then returned to their rebellion. Still, God sent Nahum, as both a hope for the Israelites and a final warning for the Assyrian people. God could have destroyed Nineveh on the spot without a word, but instead He pursued friendship one more time. In the end the Assyrians decided their rebellion toward God was the best move, but God still desired their friendship.

When God seeks friendship from people who are in rebellion, He does so through opposition. This is why so many people find God after they have hit bottom. As a pastor I have talked to hundreds of people over the years who have found God in the middle of their desperation. We often say that people hit rock bottom and look up to find God, but maybe God takes people to the bottom so that He can befriend them there.

What does friendship with God require of us? First, it requires belief. The book of James recalls a story about Abraham from the First Testament.

"And the scripture was fulfilled that says, 'Abraham believed God, and it was credited to him as righteousness, and he was called God's friend.'" **James 3:23**

To be friends with God, we have to fully believe in Him. For us, that means we must believe in the Second Testament condition for friendship:

"For God so loved the world that He gave His one and only Son, that whoever believes in him shall not perish but have eternal life. For God did not send His Son into the world to condemn the world, but to save the world through Him." **John 3:16-17**

Jesus is God's blanket offer of friendship for the world. Belief in Jesus as the way to God guarantees that, while God might still be against our actions, He will never be against us to the point of destruction.

Second, friendship with God requires surrender. Eugene Peterson translates Jesus' words this way:

Then Jesus went to work on His disciples. "Anyone who intends to come with me has to let me lead. You're not in the driver's seat; I am." **Matthew 16:24**

To be friends with God, we must surrender our lives completely to the plan of God through Jesus. This action is important because rebellion is our dominant natural tendency. We like to do things our way, in our time, and for our benefit. We want to be in charge.

My niece Hayley is a very stubborn toddler. When she crosses the line, my sister puts her in the "time-out chair." This chair sits in the kitchen while the microwave timer counts down Hayley's time-out minutes. About half way through a recent session in the time-out chair, Hayley looked both ways to make sure the coast was clear and loudly exclaimed, "BEEP!" She then excused herself from time-out.

We just don't like someone else calling the shots.

Surrender to Jesus means that we lay aside everything—all competing ambitions, allegiances, and affections. It means that we join with Him in the restoration of the world through service and mission. We relax our grip on our money, our careers, our families, and everything else so that Jesus can be lifted high in our lives. Surrender is not easy, but it is absolutely necessary to become a friend of God.

God has always desired our friendship, even enough to stand against us at times. If we believe in and surrender to God through Jesus, we can be certain that our friendship request will never be denied.

CHAPTER 12:
Predators

"Where now is the lion's den
> The place where they fed their young,
Where the lion and lioness went,
> And the cubs, with nothing to fear?
The lion killed enough for his cubs
> And strangled the prey for his mate,
Filling his lairs with the kill
> And his dens with the prey." **Nahum 2:11-12**

The Assyrians were obsessed with lions. The national symbol of Assyrian dominance was the lion. The palace of King Ashurbanipal was decorated with wall carvings of his lion hunts. They even imported lions to the royal preserves so they could hunt them. Writing of their exploits, they often depicted themselves as a lion. Nineveh was often called "the lion's den" because it was the place where people were brought and tortured publicly. Assyria loved its lions.

If you read chapter two of this book, and if you've ever watched Animal Planet, Assyria's reason for choosing the lion as a symbol seems pretty clear. Both Assyrians and lions were brutal; both killed without warning; both had no rival, and both were predators. A predator is anyone who attacks in order to get something. The Assyrians were destroying the world for their own selfish gain.

Nahum uses the passage above, commonly known as "the lion taunt," to forecast a day when the Assyrian predator would become the prey. The sarcasm of these words would not have been missed by the Assyrian King and would have brought great joy to those suffering in Israel. God was against the cruelty of the predator; their time of hunting was over. Predatory behavior is still happening around the world today, and God still stands in defense of the innocent.

Slavery and sex trafficking

In 2004 an estimated 600,000 to 800,000 men, women, and children were trafficked across international borders and forced into sex trade. Seventy percent were female, and 50 percent were children.

The number of U.S. citizens trafficked within the country each year for sex or labor is estimated at 200,000.

In the last decade, 200,000 Nepali girls, some as young as 9, have been sold into India's red-light districts.

Afghani women are sold into prostitution in Pakistan for around 600 rupees – less than $4 a pound--depending on their weight.

About 50,000 Asian, Latin American and Eastern European women and children are trafficked into the United States for sexual exploitation; the going rate is between $12,000 and $18,000 each.

Ten thousand children between the ages of 6 and 14 are in Sri Lankan brothels.

Domestic abuse of women in America

In 2009, approximately 4.8 million women reported physical abuse by a husband or partner.

One in four women will experience physical domestic abuse in her lifetime.

On average, a woman is raped every two minutes.

It is estimated that less than 20 percent of abused women report their abuse to police or seek treatment.

The health-related cost for domestically abused women is four billion dollars.

Domestic abuse of children in America

A report of child abuse is made every ten seconds.

Thirty-two percent of abused children are under four years old.

Five children die every day as a result of abuse.

Seventy-five percent of deaths by abuse are children under four years old.

Thirty percent of abused children will later abuse their own children.

Abuse of Creation

Experts believe that the recent British Petroleum oil spill will cause at least fifty years of damage to the ecosystem.

In the past ten years, ten million acres of South American rain forest were cleared to make way for cattle ranches.

America produces 230 million tons of trash a year. The trash that is not recycled contaminates drinking water and causes air pollution.

Because of the illegal poaching of animals for profit, there are more endangered species now than at any time in human history.

These statistics might not affect each of us on the same level, and an argument could be made for their order of importance. Regardless of your opinion, you should understand that they all find their root in predatory behavior. Those of us who follow Jesus have two possible responses to predators.

First, if you are a predator of people, you need to stop and make things right. Nahum shows us the level of God's anger toward those who hurt the innocent. If you are involved in any predatory practices toward another person, you need to stop, confess before God, become accountable to the law, and seek personal help. If you are not a predator, you should pause to consider how you might be indirectly involved:

> Pornography and the sex-trafficking industry are indisputably linked. If you support pornographic web sites, you are a predator.

> Physical abuse of women is much easier to track than emotional abuse. If you abuse your spouse mentally or emotionally, you are a predator.

> Many parents discipline their kids out of anger or use excessive force. If you let your anger control your parenting, you are a predator.

> Many of us have not taken the time to understand the issues facing our planet. If you refuse to become educated about issues concerning creation, you are an environmental predator.

Second, if you see predatory behavior, you need to find a way to help. Followers of Jesus shadow God as His restoration movement takes place. Consequently, if something matters to God, it should matter to us. Here are a few ways that team Jesus is working against predators:

Zach Hunter founded the organization Loose Change to Loosen Chains when he was twelve years old. Now seventeen, this anti-slavery activist has helped to raise thousands of dollars for the fight against slavery and sex trafficking.

Gary Haugen is president of the International Justice Mission, a human rights agency that secures justice for victims of slavery, sexual exploitation and other forms of violent oppression. IJM lawyers, investigators and aftercare professionals work with local officials to ensure immediate victim rescue and aftercare, to prosecute perpetrators, and to promote functioning public justice systems.

Bill McKibben is an environmentalist who founded the "Step It Up" project and *350.org* – both organizations that work to care for the planet. He was named to MSN's list of "Most Influential Men" in 2009.

Sarah Symons is co-founder of the "Emancipation Network," an organization fighting against slavery in Nepal. Sarah's unique approach helps survivors of trafficking make products that can raise money to free more victims.

I could list many other examples of followers of Jesus who are fighting against predators. In fact, each of the four mentioned above has hundreds of volunteers who allow him to make a difference. The point here is that we must find ways to work against the damage being done by predators in our world. If you have no idea where to start, read the statistics one more time. Which ones make you sad, sick, or angry? Pick an issue, do some research, and find out where you can get involved.

God is against predators. If you are one, you need to stop and repent. If you are not, you need to find a way to help the victims.

> "Religion that God our Father accepts as pure and faultless is this: to look after orphans and widows in their distress and to keep oneself from being polluted by the world." **James 1:27**

Questions for Further Reflection

1. At the Winds, we talk about shadowing God as he heals the world. What has this, "shadowing" looked like for you personally? Have you ever felt the benefits of someone who shadowed God in the world? Have you ever experienced someone who used the gospel to beat people up? How did it make you feel? In what ways are we turning the good news into "not-so-good news? How might you become more educated about God's love for all of his creation?

2. What stories have inspired you personally? Do you have a story that has helped other people? Which stories in the Bible bring you hope? Do you have any altars (things that remind you of the stories) in your life?

3. What similarities do you find between Assyria and America when it comes to money? What are the easiest ways for you to leave God out of the occasion? Would you categorize yourself as a taker, a getter, or a giver? Are you more comfortable with normal budgeting than strategic generosity? Why?

4. What are some of the ways that you might have misunderstood friendship with God? Does it bother you that friendship with God is all about Him? Why? Take some time and evaluate what you believe about God. Do your beliefs change your views about friendship with God?

5. Looking over the list of modern day predators, which one angers you the most? Have you spent any time educating yourself about the problem? What did you find? How can you be part of the solution? Are there any areas where you are contributing to predatory behavior? What can you do to make changes?

The Elements of Spiritual Formation

Something For Your Soul
SCARY STUFF – VICTIMS AND MONSTERS...

Take some concentrated time to examine these two separate areas of your life: being a victim and being the monster. Neither one is easy. No one likes revisiting pain as a victim or how it is we have hurt others.

How have you been both?

Recognize God as the One who is capable and desiring to heal you on both sides of the pain fence; as the one bruised and as the one who bruises. Healing begins when we recognize and give both sides to God. Take some time to talk with God about those aspects of your life.

Something For Your Relationships
WHAT JONAH SAID ...

Read the book in the Bible entitled Jonah, and invite some others to join you in the story (like your kids, small group or coworker). It is only four chapters long and has some great stuff to discover.

Think in pictures as you read. What do you notice and see? What do you learn about Jonah? About God? About yourself?

Something For Your Church
STORIES CREATE STORIES...

Recently someone asked why it was important for him to share his spiritual story with others. The answer: it provides hope and perspective for those hearing it. It allows others to see the movement inherent in spiritual journey; to understand what lies ahead.

Sometimes even the most insignificant of things are inspirational to others. Share your spiritual journey and let God use it to bless and encourage others. (At Westwinds, contact Becky to share your story – becky@ westwinds.org).

Something For Your World
DO SOMETHING...

Literally, www.dosomething.org. Check out the website to learn more about social justice in our world. Find an area of interest and get engaged...do something to shadow God in the world around you.

SECTION THREE
Nahum 3:1-19

Nahum Chapter Three:
The Cobblestone Translation

Woe to the city of blood –
    Full of lies,
        Crammed with wealth,
           Addicted to violence!

Hear the sound of whips and the noise of the wheels.
    Hear horses galloping and chariots clattering wildly.

Horsemen charge with bright sword and glittering spear.
    Piles of dead, heaps of corpses,
So many bodies that people stumble over them.

All because of the endless lust of the prostitute, the mistress of sorceries.
    She was charming and a lover of magic.
She hade nations slaves with her prostitution and her witchcraft.

"I am your enemy, whore Nineveh",
    Says the Lord of Heaven's armies.
"I will pull your dress up over your face
    And show all the earth your nakedness and shame."

I will pelt you with dung and make a fool of you.
>   I will make people stare at you: "Slut on exhibit!"

All who see you will shrink back and say,
>   "Nineveh is wasted. Where are the mourners?
Does anyone regret your destruction?"

Are you any better than the city of Thebes,
>   Proudly invincible on the Nile River?
The river was her defense; the waters were like a wall around her.
>   Cush and Egypt gave her endless strength; Put and Libya supported her.

But Thebes was captured and went into captivity.
>   Her babies smashed to death in public view on the streets,
Her prize leaders auctioned off, and all of her leaders put in chains.

Expect the same treatment, Nineveh.
>   You will also be drunk; you will be hidden;
You will look for a place safe from the enemy.
>   All your defenses are like fig trees with ripe fruit.
If they are shaken, they fall into the mouth of the eater.

Look at your troops _ they are women!
>   The gates of your land are wide open to your enemies;
Enemy fire will burn you up.

Get enough water before the long war begins.
Make your defenses strong!
Go into the pits to trample clay, and pack it into molds,
Making bricks to repair the walls.

But the fire will devour you; the sword will kill you.
The enemy will consume you like locusts, devouring everything they see.
There will be no escape, even if you multiply like swarming locusts.

Your traders are more than the stars in the sky.
But like a swarm of locusts,
They strip the land and then fly away.
Your commanders are like swarming locusts,
And your generals like great grasshoppers
Settling on the fences on a cold day.
When the sun comes up, they fly away,
And no one knows where they have gone.

Your shepherds are asleep, O Assyrian king;
Your princes lie dead in the dust.
Your people are scatter and lost,
And there is no one to bring them back.

There is no healing for your wound; your injury is fatal.
Everyone who hears about you will applaud.
Where can anyone be found who has not suffered from your endless cruelty?

the comfort of vengeance

CHAPTER THIRTEEN:
Mind the Gap

Everyone has a friend that is embarrassing to be around sometimes. You know the one. Every time you're with this person, you want to say to a complete stranger, "I don't really know him that well."

If you don't have a person like this in your life, guess what? You *are* that embarrassing person.

My embarrassing friend is Dale. Dale is one of my best friends. At times I wouldn't have survived without his friendship. We laugh together and cry together; I can genuinely say that I love him dearly. A worship pastor in Milwaukee, the hand of God is on his ministry and his life.

Dale is also very loud and very alive. When you go places with him, things just happen. He begins conversations with strangers, his laugh is loud and infectious, and he is noticed everywhere he goes. A few years back we went to a Minnesota Vikings football game. As it was the week before the hated Green Bay Packers came to town, the mood in the stadium was fairly tense. Dale is a die-hard Packers fan, so I made him promise not to cause a scene. I have since realized something about people like Dale. While they are very sincere in their promises not to cause you embarrassment, they lack the ability to follow through on those promises.

In the third quarter, the Vikings were struggling. Specifically, their kicker was short on the kickoffs, resulting in great field position for the other team. After the third or fourth bad kick, Dale chose a particularly quiet moment to leap from his seat and yell,

"Do your stinking job!"

A few fans mumbled approval, and I tried to pretend it hadn't happened. The next Vikings kickoff was absolutely perfect, right out of the back of the end zone. As the cheers of the crowd quieted, Dale jumped up again, turned to the rows behind him, and said,

"Don't you cheer for him; he's only doing his job! It's what he's supposed to do. No one cheers for me when I do my job!"

At this point even the intoxicated guy next to me was telling Dale to calm down. Thankfully, the game ended without any further incident. As we got up to leave our seats, however, Dale dropped one last gem on the crowd.

"I know I'm here today, but next week I'M CHEERING FOR THE PACKERS! GO FAVRE!"

We barely made it out of the stadium alive. As we ran to our car, I just kept yelling, "I really don't know him that well!"

At times we all want to distance ourselves from someone's beliefs, actions, or words. In a much more serious way, Nahum provides us with that kind of feeling. Not wanting to be associated with God's judgment against the Assyrians, we distance ourselves from the story, hoping that somehow it doesn't apply to us. Maybe you've been distancing yourself from the story as you've read the first two sections of this book.

In some ways this distance is understandable. Nahum was written to specific people in a specific time in history. God's words of judgment were directed toward Assyria in the seventh century B.C., not America in the twenty-first century. Does Nahum have anything to say to us now?

> "All scripture is God-breathed and is useful for teaching, rebuking, correcting and training in righteousness, so that the man of God may be thoroughly equipped for every good work." **2 Timothy 3:16**

Paul's words to Timothy remind us that Scripture is given for application, not just information. Our challenge as followers of Jesus living in twenty-first century America is to allow Nahum's message to speak into our lives. If we distance ourselves, we become like the Assyrians. Somewhere between Jonah and Nahum, the Assyrians decided that they were exempt from God's warnings. They distanced themselves from the message and eventually paid the price.

I want to share a few verses with you from the First Testament. The verses that follow all contain God's words of judgment toward people. See if any of them sound familiar.

> "I will pull your skirts up over your face
> That your shame may be seen."

> "Your nakedness will be exposed and your shame
> uncovered. I will take vengeance; I will spare no one."

> "Yet they rebelled and grieved His Holy Spirit.
> So He turned and became their enemy
> And He Himself fought against them."

> "I myself will fight against you
> With an outstretched hand and a mighty arm
> In anger and fury and great wrath."

You might recognize God's angry words from Nahum chapter 3. Because God was against Nineveh, He would expose their evil and would Himself fight against them. There's only one small problem.

None of these verses are from Nahum.

The above verses come from Isaiah and Jeremiah, both books written as warnings to Israel. In fact, the language of God's judgment in the First Testament almost always points at God's people. Nahum is the exception, not the rule. If we understand God's judgment towards all people, then we cannot separate ourselves from the message of Nahum We can't ever say, "I don't really know him that well." We must stand in solidarity with the judged.

So how can we stand close to the book of Nahum, inviting God to speak into our lives? We can start by developing the habit of personal evaluation. Evaluation moments happen when we ask the tough questions about our hearts and actions. Just as Ephesians 5 tells us to "not act thoughtlessly, but try and understand what God wants us to do," we should constantly be evaluating our hearts and seeing where we need to change.

I'm a fan of the show *Biggest Loser*. I am inspired by people's courage to reclaim control of their weight and ultimately their lives. Early in each season is one particularly painful moment: the first weigh in. Most contestants have no idea what they actually weigh. When they step onto the scale publicly and see their true weight for the first time, it is more than they can handle. Although this moment is incredibly difficult, contestants often point back to the first weigh-in as the pivotal moment in their experience.

As followers of Jesus, we must be willing to continually step on the "spiritual scales," inviting the Holy Spirit to convict us, and allowing our friends to speak into our lives. Like the scene from the *Biggest Loser*, these moments of evaluation can be hard and painful, but they allow us to become the people God wants us to be.

As you evaluate your life from the perspective of Nahum, you probably won't spend much time on the question, "Did I raid a neighboring town this week?" The value of evaluation is not that it always exposes something but that it never lets something stay hidden. We all have a little Assyrian in us, and we need to let the Holy Spirit change our hearts.

Each section of this book ends with discussion questions and Elements options. One way to evaluate yourself is to discuss these things with your friends. Talk about what God is teaching you. Ask your friends if they see areas in you that need to be corrected. Use these tools to hold each other accountable to the things Nahum teaches us about God and how we relate to Him.

CHAPTER 14:
The City of Blood

"Woe to the city of blood, full of lies,
    Full of plunder, never without victims!
The crack of whips, the clatter of wheels,
    Galloping horses and jolting chariots!
Charging cavalry, flashing swords and glittering spears!

"Many casualties, piles of dead, bodies without number,
    People stumbling over the corpses.

"All because of the wanton lust of a harlot,
    Alluring, the mistress of sorceries,
Who enslaved nations by her prostitution
    And people by her witchcraft." **Nahum 3:1-4**

Pop quiz time! Can you guess which major U.S. cities these nicknames represent?

Emerald City, Windy City, Music City, Motor City, Twin Cities, Sin City, Mile-High City.

If you guessed Seattle, Chicago, Nashville, Detroit, Minneapolis/St. Paul, Las Vegas, and Denver, pat yourself on the back!

I live in Jackson, Michigan, nicknamed "Birthplace of the Republican Party." While I'm not wearing that title on a t-shirt any time soon, it sounds pretty good when compared with the one Nahum gives Nineveh—"The City of Blood."

The name "City of Blood" referenced the Assyrian's violent oppression of the world, but don't let the name fool you into thinking of Nineveh as a dark and desolate place. Nineveh was absolutely breathtaking. Visiting Nineveh would have been like visiting New York; you could feel the electricity. Living in Nineveh would have also offered resources and opportunities unavailable in smaller cities. Nineveh was the greatest city in the world.

Against this backdrop Nahum leveled his most insulting words up to this point. This passage is so difficult and the words so harsh that some commentaries skip it altogether. Here is how Eugene Peterson translates Nahum's words:

> "And whores! Whores without end! Whore City, fatally seductive, you're the Witch of Seduction, luring nations to their ruin with your evil spells." **Nahum 3:1-4 (Message)**

Nahum referred to the city of Nineveh as a prostitute and a witch, the two dirtiest professions in the Ancient Near East. As my dad used to say, "Boy, them's fightin' words where I come from."

It does seem Nahum's anger finally got the best of him, but that is not the case. In fact, Nahum wasn't speaking against prostitution or witchcraft here. He used these words to explain why the Assyrians had become the "City of Blood." If Nahum were speaking our language right now, he would have said something like this:

> There are piles of dead, and no one can take a step without stumbling over a body. All of this will happen to the great Nineveh because of their complete lust for sex and money.

By calling Nineveh a prostitute, Nahum was accusing them of immorality. In the First Testament, immorality was broader than just sex; it included any worship of created things. When Nahum referred to Nineveh as a witch, he was referring to their specific use of magic. In Nineveh, sorcery was always associated with threats of blackmail and extortion. If the poor and common people believed the power of a witch, then that witch could demand anything in exchange for protection. Nahum told Nineveh that their lust for sex and money was the real motivation behind all of their actions and the real reason they would be destroyed.

Let's recap: Nineveh allowed their desires for sex and money to control their actions, resulting in suffering for the rest of the world. Does any of this sound familiar?

> In 1860 there were over four million slaves in America. We traded human lives for cheap labor and profit, hoping to sustain a way of life.

> Currently over two million people a year are trafficked around the world for sexual purposes. We are trading human life and dignity for sexual pleasure.

> Thousands of people have been killed in Sierra Leone over the mining of "conflict diamonds," which produce almost eight billion dollars a year. We are killing people in order to make money.

> In America, the pornography industry makes over three thousand dollars every second. Porn makes more money than Microsoft, Google, Amazon, eBay, Yahoo, Apple and Netflix combined. We are killing marriages and families in order to make money.

Nahum's message is as timely today as it has ever been, but we don't want to admit it. We attempt to distance ourselves from the comparison to Nineveh by arguing that we are not directly involved in evil motivated by sex or wealth. If evil decisions are made--we aren't the ones calling the shots.

This thinking brings up an interesting question. Why didn't God judge only the king of Assyria? The reason, of course, is that the king did not act alone. While certainly some Assyrians had stayed true to Jonah's message of repentance, the majority were contributing indirectly to Assyria's reign of evil. In God's eyes these people were just as guilty as the king. The city of Nineveh was filled with people who had never killed anyone but who were still enjoying a culture driven by sex and money.

Today we can still be motivated by sex and money in ways that are definitely "under the radar." As followers of Jesus, we need to search our lives for anything based on these bad motives. Here are some examples to consider:

> The average American family carries about fifteen thousand dollars of debt, not including their mortgage. Our debt is one factor that keeps us from investing ourselves generously in issues around the world. We are making decisions motivated by money and not by our values.

> Marital affairs are the second leading cause of divorce in America. Roughly twenty-five percent of men claim to have had an affair. Seventy percent of men admit to viewing pornography. We are making decisions motivated completely by sexual desire and not by our marriage vows.

> The average father spends less than two hours per day (not counting sleep) in the same physical location as his child. We are making decisions motivated by our desire to make more money, not by our commitment to family.

We are more like the people of Nineveh than we care to admit. In order to be different, we must stop being controlled by bad motives and return to God's way of living in the world. You might think of this as repentance; a word that literally means "to return."

We have to spend more wisely.

We have to be faithful to our marriages.

We have to invest time in our children.

We have to live differently than the culture around us.

"So put to death the sinful, earthly things lurking within you. Have nothing to do with sexual sin, impurity, lust, and shameful desires. Don't be greedy for the good things of this life, for that is idolatry. God's terrible anger will come upon those who do such things."
Colossians 3:5 (NLT)

CHAPTER 15:
Naked Judgment

"I am against you," declares the Lord Almighty.
>   I will lift your skirts over your face.
> I will show the nations your nakedness
>   And the kingdoms your shame.
> I will pelt you with filth,
>   I will treat you with contempt
> And I will make you a spectacle." **Nahum 3:5-6**

I have a friend who always "crosses the line," if you know what I mean. He consistently takes things one step too far with a joke or a comment, always leaving me feeling a little bit uncomfortable. In these verses Nahum seems to have crossed some pretty big lines. In fact, these might be the most uncomfortable words in the Bible. Considering some of the other words in the Bible, that's saying something. As my friend Brooke said after reading Nahum, "I don't know if I want to read this part of the Bible any more."

Before we look at what Nahum was saying, we must understand what he was not saying. This passage is not about women, not even a little bit. Nahum was speaking directly to the nation of Assyria as a whole. In ancient literature, cities were commonly referred to as women (see Nahum 2:10 and 3:8-10). Nahum's metaphor about the "lifting of skirts" is a taunt against Assyria, not against women. In light of the horrific abuse of women around the world, it is very important to understand Nahum's meaning.

If Nahum wasn't referring to literal women here, what was he saying? How do you lift the skirts of a city? Eugene Peterson's translation says it this way:

"I'll strip you of your seductive silk robes and expose you on the world stage. I'll let the nations get their fill of the ugly truth of who you really are and have been all along." **Nahum 3:5 (Message)**

Nahum was threatening Assyria with the judgment of God. God was going to expose Nineveh for what they really were, and the process was going to be shameful. The thought of Assyria, the most powerful empire in the world, suffering shame was hard to believe. Yet Nahum promised that God's judgment of Assyria would humiliate them just as if they had been publicly exposed. Apparently, God's judgment is no walk in the park.

But wait—there's more...

Apparently God's judgment wasn't exclusively reserved for Assyria. We know this because of what Nahum said next:

> "Are you better than Thebes, situated on the Nile, with water around her? The river was her defense, the waters her wall. Cush and Egypt were her boundless strength; Put and Libya were among her allies. Yet she was taken captive and went into exile." **Nahum 3:8-10a**

Nahum threatened Assyria by bringing up the recent destruction of Thebes, the capital city of ancient Egypt. The irony here is that Assyria was the nation that destroyed Thebes. Nahum was telling the Assyrians that just as God allowed them to destroy Thebes, God would bring someone along to destroy them.

But wait—it gets even worse...

Apparently God's judgment wasn't exclusively reserved for the bad guys. Here's a quick list of the Biblical prophets who spoke of God's judgment on His own people, Israel: Isaiah, Jeremiah, Ezekiel, Hosea, Amos, Micah, Habakkuk, Zephaniah, and Malachi. God judged the bad guys, but He also judged the good guys. He used the same language, the same consequences, and in some places, the same people.

Paul then tells us that everyone will face this judgment from God.

> "It is written: 'As surely as I live, says the Lord, every knee will bow before me; every tongue will confess to God.' So then each of us will give an account of himself to God." **Romans 14:11-12**

What does it mean for us to be judged by God? We can start by making a distinction between judgment now and judgment later. Paul spoke of a judgment that is coming in the future, a final judgment, if you will. This is the judgment the writer of Hebrews referenced when he said, "It is destined that each person dies only once and after that comes judgment." This judgment is waiting for each person at the end of life, and it is final and complete.

We might think of present judgment differently. Because of the work of Jesus on the cross, our judgment has been suspended. (We will explore this idea thoroughly in the next chapter.) Bishop Tom Wright refers to judgment now as "judgment by nature." In other words, we are judged in this life *by* our sin, and not *for* our sin.

> As I was writing this chapter, my wife called. She had just received a speeding ticket. While speeding tickets stink, we did not think of this as the judgment of God on her life. Instead, we understood that, not paying attention, she had driven too fast. The ticket was a result of her actions, not the abstract judgment of God.
>
> I have a very young friend who became pregnant outside marriage and then quickly married the father of her unborn child. Soon after their marriage, she discovered he was not the person he had claimed to be. She has since dealt with the pain of divorce, having her first child, single parenthood, and humiliation. While some might view

these things as the judgment of God, we better understand them as "natural judgment." God didn't make her pregnant or suddenly make things true about her ex-husband. The pain she felt was a result of her actions, not the intentional punishment of God.

We will be judged for our sin eventually, every one of us. For now, we believe that final judgment has been suspended through Jesus. When we live apart from God in this life, the consequences are largely a natural part of our world.

A common question is, "What will this final judgment look like?" As we discussed previously, our bad images of God sometimes lead us to bad conclusions about God. The same is true when we think about judgment.

> We think God's judgment is like standing in front of Judge Judy and learning what our penalty is. Maybe God has a gavel and a hatred for being interrupted.

> We think God's judgment is like standing in front of Simon Cowell and hearing how bad we are. Maybe God has a British accent and a sweet V-neck.

While no one knows for sure what our judgment will look like, Scripture seems to indicate something far worse than a critique of our song choice.

"Then I saw a great white throne and Him who was seated on it. Earth and sky fled from His presence, and there was no place for them. And I saw the dead, great and small, standing before the throne, and books were opened. Another book was opened, which is the book of life. The dead were judged according to what they had done as recorded in the books."
Revelation 20: 11-12

This judgment will be not only difficult but incredibly thorough. Listen to Jesus' words in Matthew:

> "But I tell you that men will have to give account on the day of judgment for every careless word they have spoken."
> **Matthew 12:36**

We are judged for every careless word, so (based on my drive to work this morning) I'm in a lot of trouble. Jesus paints a picture of judgment far more comprehensive and conclusive than what we might imagine. Maybe these would be better images from our culture:

> God's judgment might be like the weigh-in on *The Biggest Loser*. We will stand alone and exposed before God. Nothing will be able to hide our deformity, and the scales of judgment will be painfully accurate.

> God's judgment might be like the 360-degree mirror room in *What Not to Wear*. We will be surrounded by the righteousness of God, and there will be no way to cover any of our flaws.

God's judgment of us will be absolutely complete. Nothing will be hidden; everything will be exposed; we will have no way to do damage control. In the words of Nahum, "Everyone will see who you really are, and have been all along." God's final judgment is for everyone, and we all have it coming. How in the world can any of us survive?

That is a great question…

     with a great answer…

          in the next chapter.

CHAPTER 16:
There's Still Hope

"'No wonder I am your enemy!'
　　　Declares the Lord Almighty.
'And now I will lift your skirts
　　　So all the earth can see your nakedness and shame.
I will cover you with filth
　　　And show the world how vile you really are.
All who see you will shrink back in horror.'"
Nahum 3:5-6 (NLT)

"God made him who had no sin to be sin for us, so that in him we might become the righteousness of God." **1 Corinthians 5:21**

"The Lord is good, a refuge in times of trouble.
　　　He cares for those who trust in him." **Nahum 1:7**

As a kid, I used to watch the old *Batman* show with Adam West. Each show was thirty minutes long, but each episode always spanned two days. The first half would set up the story, always ending with Batman and Robin caught in an evil villain's trap. Just when I was ready to see how they escaped, the narrator would come in with a series of questions:

"Is this the end for the dynamic duo?"

"Will the Riddler take over Gotham City?"

"Will Batman's true identity be revealed?"

Then the narrator would give his famous sign off line: "Find out tomorrow… same Bat time…same Bat channel." If you were (as I was) eight years old, the only thing that mattered was what happened next.

We left the last chapter with the picture of humanity standing exposed in judgment before God. We asked the question, "How can anyone survive?"

The answer is Jesus.

The work of Jesus on the cross allows us to survive the judgment of God. However, we should understand that the cross does not cancel our judgment. Scripture is clear that we will all be judged. But the cross guarantees that final judgment does not have to end in punishment. In the last chapter, we discussed Nahum's image of people exposed in judgment. In that light, listen to Paul's words in Galatians and Colossians:

> "You are all sons of God through faith in Christ Jesus, for all of you who were baptized into Christ have clothed yourselves with Christ. There is neither Jew nor Greek, slave nor free, male nor female, for you are all one in Christ Jesus." **Galatians 3:26-28**

> "Don't lie to each other, for you have stripped off your old evil nature and all its wicked deeds. In its place you have clothed yourselves with a brand-new nature that is continually being renewed as you learn more and more about Christ, who created this new nature within you. In this new life, it doesn't matter if you are a Jew or a Gentile, circumcised or uncircumcised, barbaric, uncivilized, slave, or free. Christ is all that matters, and He lives in all of us." **Colossians 3:9-11 (NLT)**

Picture this: You are standing backstage in an empty arena, completely naked. For whatever reason, you are required to walk onto the stage to face a single judge. As you wait for your name to be called, you sneak a glance into the mirror and realize that the years have not been kind. There is no possible way for you to suck in one part while sticking out another. The time has come; you walk out onto the stage with your eyes on the ground. As you await the judge's response, you finally make eye contact. He has the biggest smile you have ever seen. You can't imagine why he is being so gracious in light of your appearance. With that thought, you catch a glimpse of yourself. You are not naked. Instead, you are wearing the most beautiful clothes imaginable. No outfit has ever fit you this well, and the judge can't stop smiling.

Jesus is your outfit.

Judgment says we will be exposed in our sin and shame. The cross says that when our skirts are lifted, Jesus will be the only thing God sees. Jesus takes away our shame. This rescue from the violence of judgment is precisely why Jesus had to die such a violent death. The cross wasn't just a token sacrifice; it was all of God's judgment and anger toward the world, dropped like a bomb on one person. Isaiah prophesied about the death of Jesus this way:

> "Surely He took up our infirmities and carried our sorrows, yet we considered Him stricken by God, smitten by Him, and afflicted. But He was pierced for our transgressions; He was crushed for our iniquities; the punishment that brought us peace was upon Him, and by His wounds we are healed." **Isaiah 53:4-5**

If we learn anything about God the Father in Nahum, it's that He's not like the Jesus-part of the Trinity. His love for us can't tolerate our ignorance of Him. Our sin, even the little bits, makes Him angry enough to judge us by His perfect standards. When it comes to God, there is no such thing as a mulligan, a free pass, or a do-over. We have to get it right the first time. Of course, this isn't humanly possible. We've already messed things up in more ways than we can remember. This absolute helplessness and inability to stand in front of God on our own is what brought Jesus to the cross.

> "But in our time something new has been added. What Moses and the prophets witnessed to all those years has happened. The God-setting-things-right that we read about has become Jesus-setting-things-right for us. And not only for us, but for everyone who believes in him. For there is no difference between us and them in this. Since we've compiled this long and sorry record as sinners (both us and them) and proved that we are utterly incapable of living the glorious lives God wills for us, God did it for us. Out of sheer generosity He put us in right standing with Himself. A pure gift. He got us out of the mess we're in and restored us to where he always wanted us to be. And he did it by means of Jesus Christ."
> **Romans 3:21-24 (Message)**

Jesus didn't only take our shame on the cross; he took our sin as well. His death made it possible for us to have a second, third, and trillionth chance. He stood in our place so that we could survive judgment. Why? Why did Jesus stand in our place and take the full dose of God's anger and judgment? The answer might surprise you.

Jesus came because the Father told him to come.

> "Jesus replied, 'I assure you, the Son can do nothing by himself. He does only what he sees the Father doing. Whatever the Father does, the Son also does. For the Father loves the Son and tells him everything He is doing, and the Son will do far greater things than healing this man. You will be astonished at what He does."
> **John 5: 19-20**

"For God so loved the world that he *gave* his one and only Son, that whoever believes in him shall not perish but have eternal life." **John 3:16**

The book of Nahum, with all its judgment and violence, might make it easy to forget the extent of God's love. We might even be tempted to think of God and Jesus playing "bad cop – good cop." This is really bad theology. God sent His only Son into the world to face our judgment for one reason; because He knew that without it, we would never survive.

> "The Lord is not slow in keeping His promise, as some understand slowness. He is patient with you, not wanting anyone to perish, but everyone to come to repentance." **2 Peter 3:9**

So what do we do with all of this? First, we believe it. We put our hope and trust in Jesus' work on the cross. We understand that we deserve to face God's judgment, but Jesus has taken our place. We were naked, and He became our clothes. Jesus can only stand in our defense if we put our faith in what He has done.

> "For if you confess with your mouth that Jesus is Lord and believe in your heart that God raised Him from the dead, you will be saved." **Romans 10:9 (NLT)**

> "For anyone who calls on the name of the Lord will be saved." **Romans 10:13 (NLT)**

> "He saved us, not because of the good things we did, but because of his mercy." **Titus 3:5 (NLT)**

Second, we take our sin very seriously. Though the cross means we are forgiven, it does not mean we are no longer accountable. We must follow the way of Jesus in our actions, being quick to make things right when we sin. Dr. Tony Campolo says that since Jesus took all sin (past, present, and future) on the cross in one moment, we must think of our sin as placing him back on the cross today. The way we live does matter.

A very practical way to take sin seriously is through our practice of the Eucharist. For many of us, the Eucharist (which means "good gift") has become a pretty routine ritual. Paul warned us not to take the Eucharist lightly, but to examine ourselves as we remember the sacrifice of Jesus. This examination invites God's judgment into our hearts. Knowing that the cross has saved us, we can allow God through His Holy Spirit to expose our brokenness. As God brings our nakedness to light, we remember the good gift of Jesus, thanking Him for His work on the cross.

In the book of Exodus, God was preparing to judge Egypt with the last of the ten plagues. In preparation for God's judgment, the people of Israel were given the curious command to put blood on the top and sides of their door frames. God promised that He would not judge any house with the bloody front door.

Then God said something very interesting. He told Israel that while the Egyptians were screaming for mercy because of His judgment, the people of Israel would be peaceful and quiet. God said that if they had the blood on their door, their dog wouldn't even bark when the judgment of God passed by. Why, with the judgment of God completely surrounding them, were the Israelites told that even their Chihuahuas wouldn't be disturbed?

The blood speaks.

When God's judgment came to a house with blood on the door, no word needed to be said: the blood said it all. In the same way, when Jesus died on the cross, his blood spoke on our behalf.

There is no hope in judgment, even for the best of us. Our only hope comes in the work of Jesus on the cross. His blood spoke the final word on our behalf.

We don't have to say anything else.

> "When we were utterly helpless, Christ came at just the right time and died for us sinners. Now, no one is likely to die for a good person, though someone might be willing to die for a person who is especially good. But God showed his great love for us by sending Christ to die for us while we were still sinners. And since we have been made right in God's sight by the blood of Christ, He will certainly save us from God's judgment." **Romans 5:6-9**

CHAPTER 17:
When God Plays Taps

"O king of Assyria, your shepherds slumber;
>   Your nobles lie down to rest.
> Your people are scattered on the mountains
>   With no one to gather them.
> Nothing can heal your wounds; your injury is fatal.
>   Everyone who hears the news about you
> Claps his hands at your fall, for who has not felt
>   Your endless cruelty?" **Nahum 3:18-19**

These last two verses of the book are a funeral dirge, as in the song that gets played at a military funeral. Nahum is playing "Taps" for Assyria. Their time is up; the funeral has begun.

One hundred fifty years before Nahum, Jonah told Assyria that their time was running out, and they had listened for a while. But when Nahum brought the message again, they didn't pay any attention. Why should they? At the top of their game, nothing could possibly go wrong. Except that it did go wrong. As little as twenty years after Nahum spoke these words, the Medes and Babylonians destroyed Nineveh. Their time was up, and they never saw it coming.

The end is always coming. For over two hundred thousand people in the world, the end came today. Whether you are Assyria or Israel, you must know that eventually your time will be up. And we don't have to focus only on death here. Eventually your time will be up working your job, studying at your school, hanging with your friends, raising your kids. Your time might be up soon, and you'll probably never see it coming.

You might find yourself waiting expectantly for a change to come. Maybe you are single, ready for that condition to end. Maybe you hate your job, wanting the end to come quickly.

You also might find yourself dreading the coming change. Maybe your kids are growing up too fast, and you don't want this season to end. Maybe your company is laying people off, and your job might be ending soon.

You might even find yourself dealing with the change of death. Maybe you've lost someone recently, and you're struggling with how to handle the end. Maybe someone close to you is sick, and you're terrified about when the end will come.

In every one of these scenarios, we can come to a singular conclusion: what we do really matters.

How you treat people today matters.

How you invest your money today matters.

How you spend your time today matters.

Your funeral song is being written as you read these words, and you need to understand that what you know won't make the lyrics. This song is written completely about what you do and what you say. This is why Jesus makes a point to tell us we will be held accountable for the careless words we speak. Our actions determine the words to this song.

The question is, when the end comes for you, what will your funeral song be?

When your job ends, will you have given it your best?

When you leave high school, will your teachers be sad to see you go?

When your kids leave, will they know how much you love them?

When your spouse dies, will your faith in Jesus stay strong?

Nahum's vision of Assyria's funeral song was the nations cheering at the destruction of Nineveh. Everyone had felt Assyria's cruelty, and no one would be sad that they were gone. We need to work hard for a better ending than this one.

If God had someone like Nahum write your funeral song, what would it say? This is the question all of us need to ask.

Two great people come to mind as I think about ending well. The first is my mom. Her time was up five years ago, and to this day she is the best person I've ever known. She was crippled and suffered from a wide variety of related medical problems, but she never complained. She loved people, life, and Jesus. Mom's faith was the strongest I've ever seen. Her viewing and funeral drew hundreds of people who had been inspired by her life. When the end came, her funeral song was beautiful.

The second was my friend and mentor Randy Shafer. Randy's time here ended two years ago after a battle with cancer. He taught me so much about ministry and family. As Randy was a pastor for a long time, his life touched thousands of people. At his funeral, the Winds was filled with people who had been impacted by his ministry. His funeral song was magnificent.

My mom died suddenly, while Randy knew his story was ending. But neither of them had to scramble to rewrite their closing numbers. Their actions had been true to the message of Jesus for a long time – and their funeral songs reflected that faithfulness.

We all want our lives to count in some way, but it takes really hard work to make that happen. The challenge to live differently begins right now, in this moment, with each of us as individuals. Our funeral song is being written, and the stakes could not be any higher.

"As for me, my life has already been poured out as an offering to God. The time of my death is near. I have fought the good fight, I have finished the race, and I have remained faithful. And now the prize awaits me – the crown of righteousness that the Lord, the righteous judge, will give me on that great day of His return. And the prize is not just for me but for all who eagerly look forward to his glorious return." **2 Timothy 4:7**

Questions for further reflection

1. What part of Nahum makes you the most uncomfortable? Do you find yourself wanting to say, "This is not for me?" What role does accountability play in allowing Nahum to speak to you? How do you find accountability in your life? Who do you trust enough to give access into your life?

2. In what ways have you seen our culture influenced by sex or money? How might we be making decisions that are indirectly affected by sex or money? Do you need to return to God's best desires for you in any areas related to sex or money?

3. What comes to mind when you think of the judgment of God? Do you ever feel judged by God now? What makes you feel that way? How does your idea of God's love fit with your idea of God's judgment? How does the thought of final judgment make you feel? Scared? Angry? Guilty? Hopeless?

4. Take a minute and reflect on Jesus' death on the cross. How does His sacrifice make you feel? Does the idea that God sent Jesus to the cross change your perception of God? How? Does the seriousness of Jesus' death change how you view the Eucharist? What might you try to keep the Eucharist meaningful?

5. Does your perspective change when you realize that everything in life ends eventually? Who do you know personally that has written a great life song? What have they done specifically? Living a great life is very difficult. What things can you do to live well now? How do we make God into a, "human god"? What role does trust play in your relationship with God? Where is trusting God specifically difficult for you?

The Elements of Spiritual Formation

Something For Your Soul
OUT OF THE MESS...

Read Romans 3:21-24 in a translation that is comfortable for you. We suggest the Message or New Living translation if you are starting out (you can find these versions on line at www.biblegateway.com).

Read through the verses several times. Become very familiar with it. What is it saying to you? What questions do you raise because of what you are reading? What implications does it have upon how you think and live?

We encourage you to journal your thoughts and interactions with the text.

Something For Your Relationships
FORGIVENESS = REVENGE. WAIT..., WHAT?

Read Romans 12:17-21 several times (see above note on translations and where to find online). What are your thoughts and experiences in practicing forgiveness? Have you ever given it? Received it from someone else? Does it seem weird to think that it could be revenge? What does God mean in this passage?

Examine your heart. Ask God to seek it and know it and then reveal to you how and to whom you should grant forgiveness. Set it in motion knowing that it is an extension of how you understand and know that God has forgiven you.

Something For Your Church
COMMUNION UNION...

When is the last time you decided to hold off on communion because you first needed to go and make something right, like asking for forgiveness or granting it? The Bible says that that is when our time with God is most pure and when communion is as it should be.

The next time you have opportunity to take communion, STOP and consider the meaning of the experience. If you need to make something "right," do it first. Then come back and celebrate with a grateful heart God's gift and goodness through Jesus Christ.

Something For Your World
RESTORATION LIFESTYLE...

How are you part of the restoration movement of God in the world? Are you preserving and restoring or simply consuming, possibly abusing?

Does your lifestyle in any way support the dehumanizing of others (i.e. pornography, human trafficking directly and/or indirectly)? If so, you need to stop and seek help. Your life will never find the sense of peace you long for until your actions turn to benefit rather than demean others.

Your best source of strength in the endeavor to engage a lifestyle of restoration is the RESTORER Himself, GOD. Start with an honest conversation and then start exploring who He is and what He does.

CONCLUSION

If we're honest, most of us just want a God that we can understand. We want a God who thinks like us, talks like us, decides like us, and loves like us. We want a demi-god. A demi-god is a mythological half-god. He is better than human, but not quite as good as a full God. He's good enough to handle small or simple issues, but pretty useless against the big and complicated issues of life.

You wouldn't think that anyone would want a God who can't handle our problems, but we do. We consistently shy away from a God powerful enough to handle the biggest issues of life. Why do we walk away from a God who acts like a God?

We don't trust Him.

At the end of the day, we do not trust a real God. As much as we want a God who can be present in our hardest moments, we want control of those moments just a little bit more. We don't want to let go, but here's the reality.

Being God is harder than it looks.

As much as we try to control things, we have absolutely no control. The world is overrun by every kind of evil imaginable. Not only is it impossible to determine who's good and who's evil; we wouldn't know what to do with them if we figured it out. And what about death? Sickness? Disease? Disaster? Even at our best, we have absolutely no answer. Demi-gods have nothing to offer us.

We need the real thing. We need a God who is actually God enough to perfectly love, judge, and rule the world He created. We need a God who will judge us and save us all through the persons of His perfect Trinity. We need a God who is all God. Will this God occasionally work beyond our understanding? Absolutely. Will this God sometimes move in ways that seem unfair by human standards? You bet He will. But if we choose to trust Him, this Comforting Avenger will offer us the one thing that we cannot find anywhere else:

Hope.

Hope in His perfect love.

Hope in His perfect judgment.

Hope in His perfect Son.

God is not who you've imagined Him to be.

He's more…much more.

RESOURCES

The NIV Application Commentary by Dr. James Bruckner

The Books of Nahum, Habakkuk, and Zephaniah by O. Palmer Robertson.

Nahum: A New Translation with Introduction and Commentary by Dr. Duane L. Christensen

Reading the Old Testament: An Introduction by Lawrence Boadt

Minor Prophets, The: An Exegetical and Expository Commentary by Thomas McComiskey

Nahum by Dr. Klaas Spronk

The Diety Formerly Known as God by Jarrett Stevens

The Case for God by Karen Armstrong

The Reason for God: Belief in an Age of Skepticism by Timothy Keller

the comfort of vengeance

LaVergne, TN USA
20 January 2011
212853LV00004BA/4/P